SLAYING YOUR FEAR

A GUIDE FOR PEOPLE WHO GRAPPLE WITH INSECURITY

ADAM LANE SMITH

Copyright © 2019 by Adam Lane Smith

All rights reserved. No part of this publication may be reproduced, distributed, or transmitted in any form or by any means, including photocopying, recording, or other electronic or mechanical methods, without the prior written permission of the author, except in the case of brief quotations embedded in critical reviews and certain other noncommercial uses permitted by copyright law. Any questions can be sent to the author at Info@AdamLaneSmith.com.

The contents of this book do not guarantee success in marriage or any other relationship, should not be used to diagnose disorders, and are not intended to replace traditional mental health treatment. If you believe you are experiencing a mental health issue, please seek professional help.

This book contains sections which are works of fiction. Names, characters, businesses, places, events and incidents are either the products of the author's imagination or used in a fictitious manner. Any resemblance to actual persons, living or dead, fictional persons, or actual or fictional events is purely coincidental.

Formatting by Kevin G. Summers.
Proofreading by Jeff Hasz.

To the many dear friends who have
approached me with their secret insecurities.
May this book answer your questions better
than my fumbling on-the-spot attempts.

NEW AUTHOR FOREWORD

I didn't expect Slaying Your Fear to get this much attention.

At the time I wrote it, I was a Licensed Marriage and Family Therapist working in a clinic. And like most psychotherapists, adult attachment had not been part of my six years of schooling or three years of licensure. So when I started noticing attachment issues under the majority of other diagnoses, especially the extreme traumas I was used to treating with my PTSD specialty, I needed an easier way to talk to my clients about it.

This book in your hands is the result of that need. I wrote this short guide so I could hand it to clients after the first session and say, "Here's your main diagnosis, but the underlying issue is probably attachment. Read this short book and come back."

It's amazing to me that the guide I wrote has received such a response. Mental health professionals write to me and say they're using it to treat patients at their clinic. Program directors tell me they've introduced it as part of their curriculum for recovery or training for new professionals. Thousands of readers have written in to tell me Slaying Your Fear changed their life and their whole family as they've all adopted healthier behaviors.

As the book went viral, entertainers and industry media groups pulled me on their programs to talk about my work with attachment. And as that took off, individuals from around the world contacted me for treatment. I had to deny every request for the first few years because of the limitations of my license. In the US, psychotherapist licensure in one state only allows you to see clients in that state. Any individual in the other 49 states or territories are not allowed to receive treatment from you. And international work is impossible. Even coaching is effectively banned as it's treated like therapy and governed by the same strict controls.

With the discussion around attachment heating up and so many people begging me to work with them, I finally made the decision to terminate my psychotherapy license. That choice was gut-wrenching, because the license alone requires nine years of investment. But the ability to coach individuals in all 50 states plus every country in the world made the decision for me.

Since that moment, I've taken my attachment work internationally. And I've joined other colleagues who openly question the narrative that attachment is "just for kids." We've had fantastic discussions on many social media platforms that draw in audiences who want to learn and engage with this topic they've never heard about but which has defined most of their life and struggle.

My own approach has evolved since writing this book. In the pages ahead you'll read about my work with corrections and clinics and couples and millionaires. My work has since expanded to offering hundreds of free video guides on Youtube, streaming live on

TikTok several times a week to teach a wide audience, opening a discord community called the Attachment Circle for people serious about improving their relationships, and offering consultations to individuals all over the world. I am grateful to be allowed to help so many people and take part in their journey. It is both humbling and honoring to play a part in the healing process of a global community looking for answers.

Thank you for picking up this book. You're about to learn how attachment has secretly shaped your life, and what you can do to build the relationships you've always wanted. I would love to hear about your experience. Please contact me on Instagram @AttachmentAdam, on Tiktok @AttachmentBro, on Twitter @TheBrometheus, and on Youtube by searching Adam Lane Smith. All my bios on those platforms also include my Linktree which can direct you to a ton of resources, courses, and free materials to enhance your attachment journey. I look forward to hearing from you.

Enjoy learning about attachment. It will become a huge part of your awareness and a big answer to your past frustrations. Your life is about to change forever.

ACKNOWLEDGEMENTS

This book represents the culmination of years of study and experience and would not be possible without many edifying encounters throughout my lifetime. The author would like to thank the many people who've contributed to his education, both formally and informally.

Cynthia Borges-O'Dell and Dr. Kenneth Huntley, who mentored me through graduate school and shaped me in my earliest days as a clinician. I would not know half of what I do now without your extensive tutelage and enormous support. Thank you for forging me in the fires of wisdom and preparing me for the work ahead.

Jesse Ellis, Laura Novitsky, Jennifer Czischke, and Jennifer Fritz, my licensure supervisors. Each of you were so incredibly different and gave me a wealth of experience from which to draw. I am indebted to each of you for your hours of patience and guidance.

And the many clients I have worked with over the years, who trusted me to assist them in rebuilding their lives and finding solutions in the darkest of times. It is the dearest wish of my heart that I served you well.

"My friends only pretend to like me."

I'm sitting in my office on a Tuesday afternoon and talking with a client. She's a young woman dressed in business casual on her lunch break from work, but I've heard these words from hundreds of other clients. They may be male or female, old or young, black or white or polka-dot. The one constant is that they're consumed with crippling insecurity and can't imagine deserving to be loved.

"What makes you think they're pretending?" I ask.

She sighs. "I don't know. I'm just such a burden. How could they not hate me?"

"Have they ever given you reason to believe that? Said something? Thrown a brick at you?"

The joke does the trick and she laughs, but it's only half-hearted. Her self-loathing is weighing her down today. "No. They're too nice to do that. It's just a feeling I have."

"Have you ever tested it?"

She shoots me a look that tells me my question sounded stupid.

"Okay," I press, "so how do you know?"

The client looks confused, but quickly settles back into resignation. "I just do. How could anyone really like me? There's nothing about me to like."

WHO I AM AND WHY I WROTE THIS BOOK

Insecurity is one of the most difficult internal challenges a person will face.

Humans are designed to flourish with love and acceptance. When a person fundamentally believes they are unlovable and will never be truly accepted, they begin to wither like a plant starving without sunlight. And when a person becomes so consumed with insecurity that they don't even trust themselves to find a way out of the pit of misery, a professional is often needed to help make things right again.

My name is Adam Lane Smith and I'm an LMFT, a Licensed Marriage and Family Therapist. I have a master's degree in Psychology, have apprenticed under 5 separate clinicians with a range of different licenses, and have been practicing individual, family, and couples therapy for years in both correctional and clinical settings.

My job is to help individuals struggling with mental health issues. Some who come in are facing simple life challenges and need encouragement and skills to get through the temporary discomfort. Others, however, are grappling with a lifelong battle against themselves. They've felt alone most of their lives and can't imagine the warmth of human acceptance. Often, this intense separation from others has left them vulnerable to a host of mental health disorders. The specific issues I see related to insecurity cover a wide range of challenges including:

- Anxiety where everything related to relationships causes the person intense fear. They are so consumed with terror about making a mistake that they wake up fearful and spend their entire day wrapped in a cloud of worry.

- Depression from a lifetime of worrying and eventual surrender to the realization that worrying does nothing to stop their pain. Nothing helps, and they succumb to learned helplessness.
- Post-traumatic Stress Disorder from a seemingly uncomplicated event which impacted the client much deeper due to their emotional isolation and latent fear.
- Relationship issues where the couple is at odds over seemingly insignificant issues, but underneath the veneer of love is a mess of terror and insecurity.

Despite the range of issues facing individuals who come in for therapy, one problem has repeatedly presented itself in my office: People who are fundamentally convinced they cannot be loved and will be abandoned for the slightest mistake. For these individuals, every day is another gauntlet of events designed to cause them to stumble and reveal the horrifying secret of just how awful they really are. Everyone they love will gasp with shock, which will quickly turn to disgust. Word will spread to everyone who ever knew the insecure individual, and by the end of the day they will be a social pariah, living under a bridge with only flea-bitten coyotes for companions.

Time and again I encounter individuals with this exact issue, and it's become prevalent enough that a recognizable pattern has emerged. People with early childhood struggles which impact their attachment style rarely seem to recover on their own. Instead, their lives seem to follow a trajectory passing through anxiety into depression, and possibly later into panic attacks, trauma, or other mental health issues.

Even older people in their sixties and seventies are sometimes afflicted by this pattern of behavior. Clients as young as 12 report the same issues, and parents I treat tell me they recognize some of the behaviors in their own tiny children at home. And once we dig into the past history of behavior, a few shared features usually come to light:

- Insecure individuals don't know how to explicitly ask others for what they want.
- When directed to state clearly what they want from others, insecure individuals experience a surge of anxiety which stops them.
- Insecure individuals suffer from low self-esteem but can't say why. They describe themselves as human garbage but can never state a compelling reason.
- Social situations are often terrifying for insecure individuals. It may seem bizarre to some that the closer they get to others, the greater the fear they experience because the stakes become so much higher.
- Insecure individuals often have few real accomplishments to their name because they tend to self-sabotage either at the

beginning or near the end of projects. They fear outcomes because they're so convinced they will screw up just before the finish line. The accomplishments they do have usually were earned because they had no choice and faced real (or perceived) severe consequences if they did not finish.

- Many insecure individuals who struggle in the above areas experienced childhood abuse and/or disruptions with their primary emotional caregivers through divorce, trauma, incest, suicide, parental abandonment, parental drug addiction, or daycare in significant quantity.

What emerges time and again are portraits of people who desperately crave love and want to keep their relationships intact at any cost, but their fear sabotages any attempt at intimacy and is causing their relationships to fail. They struggle to engage with hobbies because they never believe their work is of any worth. If writing a book, they will likely never publish it. Artwork may never see the light of day. Powering through and reaching success or sharing creations takes an act of monumental will as the insecure individual struggles mightily against their own shivering brain.

In short, these individuals face two primary issues: They struggle to attach to others in a trusting manner because they believe they are fundamentally unlovable, and they cannot accept themselves because their sense of worth is externalized to what others think of them. What others actually think of them is irrelevant, because their internal process reassures the insecure individual they can never truly be loved. Therefore, the default reaction from others who see their true selves must be disgust and rejection. Kind words, compliments, and perceived approval is at best misguided from people who don't know their secret flaws, or at worst an attempt at manipulation by people who want to hurt them. People who treat them poorly are viewed as the most honest people in the world because they at least openly acknowledge that the insecure individual doesn't deserve kindness or respect.

There is no room for love in their world. They crave love with all of their being, and they feel intense, burning affection for others, but love will always be denied to them because they refuse to accept that any love for them could ever be real.

In their own internal lives, I call these people "insecure individuals." In relationships I call them "detached."

My goal in writing this book is to create a useful resource insecure individuals and detached partners can use to navigate the tangled web of insecurity and find their way to emotional intimacy, acceptance, and fulfillment.

Slaying Your Fear will:

- Explore what insecurity feels like
- Describe the symptoms insecure individuals experience

- Explore background causes which can lead to insecurity
- Explain the impact of insecurity as it relates to the formation and severity of mental health disorders
- Provide useful tools for insecure individuals to learn to respect themselves, stop the cycle of disappointment, manage their worries, build intimate relationships, and find purpose in their lives
- Provide an example of what healthy relationships and confident living look like
- Give insecure individuals a clear roadmap to move from detached and hurting to attached and intimate

To do this, I'll be sharing stories of fictitious clients. The individuals named and described in this book are not real clients because that would be a breach of confidentiality. Every person described will instead be an amalgamation of the most common features, phrases, and situations I encounter over and over when working with insecure individuals and detached partners. Any words ascribed to the individuals have been said numerous times in my office by a variety of people.

Yes, that includes the unhappy client who opened this chapter talking about her friends secretly hating her. I've heard that precise inner struggle many times from insecure individuals who just can't believe they hold any worth at all. Overly-aggressive attempts by therapists to convince them otherwise often damage the relationship and cause the insecure individual to either believe the therapist is too stupid to recognize the client's worthlessness, or they panic because someone believes good things about them which will inevitably lead to an even worse crash when the therapist realizes how awful they truly are.

The fictitious individuals described in this book represent four of the most common insecurity presentations I work with, and they are:

Amber grew up in a dysfunctional household. Her parents are still married, but they fought constantly in front of the kids. Amber used to hide under her blankets and listen to her dad screaming at her mom. They mostly fought about his heavy drinking and the money he spent on alcohol every night at the bar. Her dad had no time for his kids and gave Amber virtually no attention. He's sober now but blames his children for not wanting to spend time with him, and her mom guilts her about staying away. In private conversations with friends, Amber calls her father a loser and her mom a stubborn victim. Now, at the age of 23, she believes she's unworthy of attention or love. She's had a couple of romantic relationships but has a hard time getting close to people, so she's alone now. Even when she is cuddling together with a partner she feels lonely. She writes fantasy novels but no one has ever read them, and she hides them away because she's certain they're worthless. She works retail but has a difficult time interacting with customers, and she finds social engagements exhausting. Her days are mostly spent sitting alone on her bed in her apartment watching anime with the door locked so her roommates won't try to speak to her.

Eric comes from a broken home. His parents divorced when he was 5 years old. He's the oldest of 3 kids and has no relationship with his father, despite his father trying to contact the children many times over the years. He blames his dad for all the family's struggles and focuses on taking care of everything his mother needs. She often leans on Eric and cries on his shoulder whenever one of her frequent boyfriends breaks up with her. One of these boyfriends molested Eric from age 7 to age 9, but he's never told anyone this because he doesn't want his mother to feel guilty. He says, "She has enough problems to deal with." Eric works as the manager of a local animal shelter because he says the animals are "more honest than people," and working alone with the dogs is the only place he ever feels at peace. Eric struggles with a team who don't seem to respect him, especially a female team leader working under him who tends to force him into giving her whatever she wants. Eric has never dated or had sex with anyone and says he has given up on romantic relationships in favor of taking care of the animals at his shelter. Eric has a few friends but struggles to stay engaged with them and constantly worries what they really think of him.

Chris grew up with a mother who worked full time and a father who worked part time. His father drank and spent most of his time out of the house, going out frequently to "handle his stress." Chris's mother never complained to Chris, but he spent his infancy and toddler years in daycare for most of every day. Much of his later childhood was spent alone when he wasn't put in charge of caring for his two younger siblings. The only guidance about sex Chris can remember his father giving him is being told, "Make sure you use a rubber, because I don't believe in abortion." At Chris's wedding, his father took him aside to tell him that "happy wife, happy life" is the only rule he needs to remember. Chris believes love must be earned and that others will forget him easily.

Ashley's father died when she was a little girl and her mother turned to heroin to manage her grief. Ashley was sexually abused multiple times by her mother's boyfriends, though she says her mother never found out. She's never had a father figure and her interactions with men prior to marriage were mostly older men molesting her, abusive boyfriends, or unwanted sexual contact with acquaintances. She was popular with the boys in high school but says women have always hated her, which is fine with her because she hates women. "I only get along with men." She's been divorced twice. When she's been married, Ashley says her interest in sex drops to almost zero and she doesn't understand why her former husbands have made such a big deal about it. Ashley fears abandonment every day and believes love must be earned by pleasing the other person and doing anything they want to keep them around.

My aim for this book is to create a guide to show a new way of living for all the insecure individuals and detached partners who need help.

Let's get started.

CHAPTER 1
Insecurity and Attachment

WHAT IS INSECURITY AND WHAT DOES IT FEEL LIKE?

If depression feels like trying to swim with weights on your ankles, insecurity feels like living in a house that's constantly experiencing earthquakes. No matter how many times you set things up they come crumbling down again, and you're constantly racing around trying to brace up things that look like they're about to fall. The floor shakes under you and wobbles your every step. Even moments of peace are frightening because you don't know when the shaking will come back twice as hard. Life is spent wondering if this is the day the ceiling finally crashes down and buries you.

Insecure people even worry about their worrying. Starting to worry sets off a reaction of nervousness about how worried they're going to become and how much of their day the worrying is going to swallow.

Apply this mental picture to every facet of life:

- Relationships
- Family
- Work

- Art
- Crafts
- Gaming
- Relaxation time
- Eating
- Sleeping

Imagine if every moment of every day was filled with some level of bubbling anxiety, constantly nagging at the corner of your mind and telling you that somewhere, something important is about to fall apart.

Imagine believing everyone who ever calls you their friend is only one realization away from rejecting you completely.

Imagine your family is your greatest source of pain. They're supposed to be the most welcoming and accepting of all the people in your life, but you never feel more alone and more resentful than you do with your family.

Imagine believing that everything important to you will fall apart at the moment of triumph and leave you disappointed and ashamed.

Insecure people don't have to imagine the above scenarios. For people with insecurity, these are real experiences in their everyday life. Moments of great joy are instead immensely fearful. Family gatherings and parties with friends feel alienating and exhausting. The slightest ambiguous word from a loved one is interpreted the worst possible way and kicks off a cycle of obsessive worrying which leads the insecure individual to run damage control before the perceived problem is even acknowledged.

In the secret core of their heart, insecure individuals believe no connection to another human being will ever be truly secure.

In the simplest terms, insecurity is a problem with attachment.

WHAT IS ATTACHMENT?

Attachment measures a person's ability to connect to other human beings.

Healthy attachment means a person connects to others with an expectation of emotional security. The person with healthy attachment does not worry they will be abandoned or forgotten because they know others will think of them even while they are apart and will make decisions with their wellbeing in mind. They do not worry when disagreements arise because they know they are connected at a deeper level. Mistakes aren't feared because the attached person knows they'll be given a chance to explain their mistake and make things right. Vulnerability is relatively easy because a person with healthy attachment believes others have their best interests at heart.

In short, a person with healthy attachment believes love is freely given instead of earned, that others love them for who they are, that people will continue to love them even in their absence, and that love cannot be casually destroyed.

Unhealthy attachment means a person struggles to believe in any emotional security, so vulnerability to others becomes dangerous and fearful. In fact, vulnerability is utterly terrifying because it could lead to judgment and abandonment as secret imperfections are revealed. Vulnerability may even lead to outright victimization by those around them. The detached person struggles constantly with worries of abandonment and being forgotten because they don't believe others really love them for who they are, only for the services they perform. They believe decisions others make will usually conflict with their own needs because the people they love don't think about them enough to remember their wellbeing, or else they just aren't important enough to consider. Disagreements and mistakes are often the end of relationships to them because they believe they'll be abandoned and rejected instantly upon displaying imperfection and will be given no chance to explain or make amends.

In short, a person with unhealthy attachment believes others only love them for the services they perform, that love must be continuously earned, that people will actively fall out of love with them every moment they are not refilling the person's pleasure meter, and that love can be accidentally destroyed by the slightest mistake.

There are many different attachment styles and attachment disorders, but for the sake of simplicity this book will stay within the realm of non-diagnosed individuals. A person can struggle with attachments without ever meeting criteria for a full diagnosis. Likewise, a person with a severe attachment issue may never be diagnosed.

With that said, people who struggle with unhealthy attachment styles often have, at the very least, attachment wounds which have fundamentally altered the way they connect to other human beings. Experts disagree on exactly when attachment styles become cemented, but studies seem to indicate that attachment develops in infants under 6 months old and continues developing throughout childhood. In fact, some experts argue that attachment styles never stop changing and growing, though it may take more effort to change as the person grows older.

WHAT DETERMINES ATTACHMENT HEALTH?

Attachment styles form as a result of the young mind trying to understand one thing: Will I be loved for who I am, or do I have to earn love?

This complicated question is boiled down to a simple black-or-white equation because the young mind is not capable of nuance. At 3 months old, an infant only knows its mother is not responding to its cries. At 3 years old, a toddler doesn't understand that daddy is hitting him because daddy has alcohol problems. At 10 years old, a little girl doesn't understand that she's been abandoned because her parents have mental health issues.

To the little mind, everything that happens is about them. Everything that happens is a direct result of the child's behavior and quality. Therefore, abuse and neglect and abandonment make the child believe:

"I deserve this."

"No one will ever treat me better than my parents, and even they couldn't love me."

"I will not be loved because I don't deserve to be loved. But maybe I can earn love if I'm good enough."

"There is something inside me that others can see, something horrible that makes it so others can't love me. I don't know what the bad thing is, so I don't know what I can't show people. I need to lock down and keep everything inside so people won't see this horrible thing and abandon me."

Any serious disruption in early life can create an attachment wound.

- Divorce, where the family is ripped apart and the child is told "sometimes love just doesn't last."

- Abuse, where the child learns they can be hurt by anyone at any time and no one will protect them

- Daycare in significant amounts and especially early in infancy, where the child is separated from their parents and must compete with others for attention and love, and where the workers change based on shifts or employment disruptions so the formed attachments disappear

- Parental neglect or emotional distance, where the child doesn't understand why their parents seem to want nothing to do with them and don't invest time or emotional energy in the child

All these occurrences can send the message to a child's brain that they are the cause for their own loneliness and that they are not worthy of being loved. As irrational as it may seem, the child's brain truly believes the parents would not get divorced and split the household if they could have loved the child enough, or that abuse would not have happened if the child was better behaved.

Usually, the child sets out on a journey to earn love from others. They become enormously eager to please and cannot say no. They are frequent targets of abuse by others because they're so desperate for approval and have no one to report abuse to.

Sometimes a detached child develops in the other direction. "If no one can love me, then screw them! I don't need their love anyway!" The child develops anger issues and avoids connection with others.

Some children may even develop a combination of both styles, avoiding connections with a cold outward persona but then becoming anxious and obsessive over the few connections they do manage to make.

What all these attachment wounds often turn into is a belief that mistreatment and misfortune is earned through behavior. Whenever something bad happens in their life, the child concludes they weren't focused enough, they weren't *worried* enough, and their latent anxiety increases.

They're also anxious because their belief is that they're utterly alone in the world. If no one can love them then they possess no emotional security at all. Anything bad can happen at any time and no one will come rescue them.

And finally, the detached child believes they can never truly earn real love because they have this secret evil thing inside of them which will make others abandon them if they relax and accidentally let the secret out.

Abandonment becomes linked to death in the child's brain. Evolutionary psychology teaches that this occurs because human brains were not formed to survive in modern urban society. Instead, our brains developed for life as it was ten thousand years ago, living in the forest and running from bears. To such a child's brain, being abandoned by both parents because the child is unlovable means they're likely going to die alone in the forest, starved or eaten or killed by strangers.

Abandonment is to be avoided at all costs. Shame and humiliation are nothing compared to abandonment, so the person with unhealthy attachment will often cast aside self-respect in a desperate bid to be loved. And when they make a mistake or perceive the other person to be abandoning them, even if it just means their phone calls haven't been answered in ten minutes, survival protocols click into action.

"You can't abandon me if I'm the one who rejects you!" the detached person screams as they send a stream of texts ending the relationship.

These initial equations about being loved versus earning love stay buried in the back of the child's mind into adulthood. Because they're the foundational building blocks of the detached person's approach to the entire world, these assumptions are never questioned or even really noticed. The detached person takes these assumptions as gospel truth and approaches every moment of their life according to the implications of their belief that they are fundamentally unlovable.

With all of that in mind, let's take a look at the background and attachment style of our four examples.

A LOOK AT OUR INDIVIDUALS

Amber's father neglected her to spend time at the bar. When he was home he mostly fought with her mother, who also had little time for Amber due to high tension and an increased workload as a functionally single parent. At age 3, Amber's brain was not equipped to understand these various factors and instead concluded that she did not get attention because she was not good enough to earn their time. Amber embarked on a journey of endless self-criticism and perfectionism in a desperate bid to tear out the part of her that makes her so unlovable.

Eric's parents divorced when he was 5 years old. Prior to this were years of tension and misery which Eric never understood. After the divorce, his mother told the three children that their dad didn't love them and didn't want to see them anymore. Whenever Eric's father tried to visit him, Eric lashed out in anger, believing he had been rejected already. As his father's inexplicable rejection sank into his mind, his mother cultivated a relationship with Eric wherein he met her emotional needs and in return she rewarded him with praise and affection. Every time Eric comforted his mother from one of her frequent breakups, they had a special mommy-son date night together. These nights were the only times Eric ever felt happy, and he learned that the more emotionally unstable his mother became, the easier it was for him to earn her attention and love.

Throughout childhood, **Chris** worried about being good enough to earn the notice of others. Anxiety built as he continued to be ignored by his parents and he assuaged this worry by focusing on caring for his siblings as the most obvious way of earning his mother's approval. Chris's young life became about service to others while denying his own needs. He could only relax when he was completely alone, but being alone reminded Chris of how desperately unfulfilled he felt.

Ashley's childhood was spent worrying about the next painful encounter she'd experience. She routinely wet her bed as a little girl to prevent her mother's boyfriends from abusing her at night. Every time she was hurt again, her worry increased as she believed she was somehow causing the incidents. By age 9 she exhibited clear Post-traumatic Stress Disorder symptoms and a massively elevated level of latent anxiety, but no one noticed.

CHAPTER 2
How does insecurity impact daily life?

TWO LEVELS OF RELATIONSHIPS

For the purposes of our discussion through the rest of this book I'm going to declare that relationships exist on two separate levels.

The top level is what I call "the fluff". These are feelings, moment-to-moment emotions people feel toward each other.

A couple may have happy fluff as they go on a date, then arrive home and realize someone has left the milk out. Now the fluff is annoyed. But the guilty partner makes up for their mistake with a foot rub. Yay, the fluff is happy again!

The fluff is not the relationship. Fluff is the feelings which spring from the relationship.

Underneath the fluff is a layer forged of pure iron. If the fluff is a cloud of feelings, the underside is the carved stone used to build monuments. I call this second layer "the framework".

The framework exists as a contract between any two individuals. Imagine, if you will, a table placed between two friends. On each side of the table is each person's needs and expectations for the relationship. At this table both friends are supposed to negotiate back and forth to get their needs met and ensure the health of their relationship, the fulfillment of their mutual goals, and so on.

When both friends have healthy attachment styles the framework develops in an open and explicit way. Throughout the life of the friendship, both will negotiate back and forth to make sure their shared goals are met and each friend stays healthy and satisfied.

Flash back a moment to the unhealthy attachment styles. Keep in mind that an individual with unhealthy attachment behaviors believes deep down there is something innately unlovable inside of them but they don't know what it is. Sharing their wants and needs risks letting the other person see this evil thing, which will inevitably lead to rejection and abandonment.

The framework, then, becomes the greatest terror.

I call insecure individuals in relationships "detached," because their attachments are so superficial and fearful. They're ready to bolt at the first sign of impending abandonment, with one foot always out the door.

If the detached person shares their needs and wants in an explicit way, they believe their friend will say, "You're not worth that! I'm out of here!" Whereupon the now ex-friend will rise from the table and bolt from the room, leaving the insecure individual abandoned and alone.

And if the insecure individual lets the other person focus on their own needs too openly, they believe the friend will stop and say, "Wait a minute, you can't meet my needs. We're done here!" Or, the person will share their needs and give the insecure individual a chance, whereupon the insecure individual will of course fail to uphold the expectations. If they could meet expectations, after all, they would never have been abandoned in the first place.

Given this sheer terror, the only remaining option is for the insecure individual to focus on the fluff while distracting both friends from the framework.

"Look how happy I can make you!" the detached person coos as they over-indulge their partner with romance, sex, compliments, and service.

"Look how happy you are!" the detached person begs as their partner starts to express dissatisfaction, confusion, and resentment.

"Look how good I can be!" the detached person shrieks as the relationship collapses and their shared goals fall to pieces.

The fluff was never meant to be the foundation of a relationship, but it's all the detached person has at their disposal to build and maintain relationships. The fluff turns into a swarm of relationships swirling around the detached person, demanding constant attention at all times. This is not just their romantic relationship, but every single relationship in their life. Parents, siblings, friends, coworkers, bosses, teachers, anyone and everyone they know. The deeper the relationship, the deeper the anxiety every time they interact.

For people with healthy attachments, every interaction is a chance to increase intimacy. For people with unhealthy attachments, every interaction is a chance to destroy everything they love.

Every day, the insecure individual must recharge the draining affection battery on each person in their life to keep the earned love flowing. Any slight mistake could cause a crash in that relationship. Being sad about losing one relationship means less energy to spend fluffing the others, which will lead to a domino cascade of erupting relationships.

In the course of one single day, the detached person believes one mistake can destroy their whole life and end with the detached person entirely alone forever.

Into this swirling maelstrom of self-loathing is dumped a number of close relationships including family, friends, and romance: foundational human relationships built on mutual sharing of needs, united goals, and trust.

Not only do the insecure individual's loved ones have needs which must be met, the detached person also has secret needs they've never shared with anyone. But people starve when their needs aren't met, and the detached person knows they need to find a way to be fulfilled.

Enter the hidden needs and unspoken transactions.

HOW CAN I GET MY NEEDS MET WITHOUT TELLING YOU WHAT THEY ARE?

The insecure individual faces the following paradox:

"I have needs, but revealing them will cause me to be abandoned. Either my loved ones will outright reject me and say, 'You're not worth this price, I'm out of here!' or else they will fulfill my need with begrudging resentment and stew on the imposition, eventually leading to abandonment later."

The detached person cannot conceive of a mindset where needs are anything but a burden to be borne. Their belief that something rotten lies deep down inside their core means their own sense of innate self-worth in a relationship is reduced to absolute zero. Their desperation to earn approval from others means the needs of others are both opportunities and burdens at the same time.

But these internal cravings are needs, not wants. Wants can be set aside but needs by their very nature must be fulfilled. Every person exists in a duality of noble cognition and ravening beast. The animal nature must be fed and has very simple needs: sustenance, shelter, pain relief, acceptance, and belonging.

What this means is that the detached person denying their needs will begin to exhibit less and less control over their behavior as their beast-self manifests more fully and searches for fulfillment. The harsh dichotomy between fulfilling their needs and dreading abandonment sparks a cognitive dissonance which pulls the detached person apart as they shred their most beloved relationships.

"I feel lonely and need us to spend more time together" twists into a passive-aggressive version which retains no vulnerability but seeks to bludgeon loved ones into meeting the need. "Oh, you're going out for lunch with your dad? You have time for everyone but me."

"I need physical intimacy and want to feel closer to you" twists into "You don't even love me anymore, I do everything right and you won't touch me."

"I made a mistake and I'm scared you'll be angry and abandon me" twists into "I wouldn't have done this in the first place if you had just [insert your favorite blame shift here]."

Paired with this onslaught of passive-aggressive attacks is the more common doormat mentality. The detached person spends most of their time in this passive, reactive state. The detached person believes they have no innate self-worth in relationships, so they must create that worth through works.

The detached person can never say no to a request from anyone they have a relationship with. The need to earn love is so overwhelming and the desperation to avoid abandonment so powerful that the concept of "no" becomes their greatest enemy. This is why insecure individuals are routinely exploited by unscrupulous abusers or addicts who latch onto them as an easy resource.

The detached person overcompensates for the lack of framework by obsessing over the fluff.

By fulfilling the perceived needs of others, the detached person is able to build temporary worth, enough to warrant a reward. The reward they want is for their needs to be met. But they'll never tell anyone their needs, and won't cop to them even if asked bluntly, "Is this what you want?"

This focus on fulfilling the needs of others in order to earn worth necessitates finding friends and partners with obvious needs and who will never run out of needs to be fulfilled. The detached person unconsciously gravitates toward the most damaged people they can find and makes projects of them as a source of perpetual approval. "If I become the one person meeting their needs over and over, they can never leave me! In fact, they'll be so grateful for my devotion that they'll meet my needs, too!"

The more damaged and broken and dangerous the person, the more enamored the detached person becomes. Their addiction to the broken person crystalizes instantly into an obsessive symbiotic bond of User and Enabler.

A damaged man is incapable of love because he does not believe love will be freely given, only earned through works. He seeks false intimacy in lust and mistakes sex for acceptance. These men seek insecure women who believe themselves unlovable and who use sex to earn approval.

And all the while, the detached person secretly resents everyone in their life for failing to meet their hidden needs. Simmering dissatisfaction stews just under the surface of their desperate clawing for approval, and this resentment explodes to the surface in patterns of frequent displays of hurtful anger, followed by a plunge deeper into doormat behavior as they fearfully seek to avoid abandonment for having lashed out.

When you're starving and you find something that's supposed to fulfill you, but it doesn't, you become desperate and gorge yourself on it. All the while, people are standing around telling you this thing you're eating is the only option. That's detached individuals in modern courtship and the rise of casual sex.

Our world is increasingly filled with damaged men and insecure women. So prevalent is this issue that many come to despair, believing this encompasses the whole of humanity. But these destructive states reflect an unnatural brokenness, not the natural state of humanity.

What all this deception and subterfuge creates is a relationship system of blind bartering where each party is trying to predict what the other side wants. When a person gets it wrong, their detached counterpart lashes out with passive-aggressive behavior to send a message through pain that the wrong exchange price was offered.

WHAT DOES DETACHMENT LOOK LIKE IN EARLY LIFE?

In childhood, insecurity may look like the kid who is always nervous about doing their homework perfectly, getting perfect grades, or being the "good kid." Obsession with perfection and devastated feelings at the smallest error are hallmarks of the detached child.

In their teens, anxiety often continues to increase and may turn to depression. As the young brain processes everything that happens to them as their own fault, the detached youth often concludes that they clearly weren't worrying *enough*. They need to worry *more* so they can dodge painful circumstances. When they run out of room to dodge and they live at an elevated level of anxiety at all times but *still* experience pain, learned helplessness usually sets in. As helplessness and hopelessness increase, depression can manifest.

The perpetual heightened level of anxiety coupled with the learned helplessness can lead to panic attacks when the detached youth experiences situations where they perceive pain or abandonment to be imminent. The fight-or-flight response recognizes that social pain and perceived abandonment are linked to death and activates when the detached person is presented with uncomfortable situations. The limbic system ignites and burns away logic and reason in an attempt to stay alive at all costs.

Other cognitive and behavioral issues may arise as well as the mind begins to crack under the constant pressure of required perfection. Believing they are alone in the world and have no control over events puts the detached person at a lowered threshold for Post-traumatic Stress Disorder. Obsessive-compulsions may take root as the detached person seeks comfort in superstition in order to gain a feeling of control over their environment. "If I click my teeth together in the correct spot exactly four times when I put on my pants, nothing bad will happen to me."

By the time the detached person reaches adulthood, they are likely to suffer from a diagnosable mental health disorder. Frequently this presents as Generalized Anxiety Disorder with a possible host of other concerns stemming from the obsessive worrying.

A LOOK AT OUR INDIVIDUALS

Amber struggled with severe anxiety as she entered her teen years. Social interaction at school was a challenge, and she was painfully shy. A few of the nicer girls tried to befriend her over the years and she mostly clung to the fringes of their social groups, but she never really had a "best friend" and wasn't invited to many sleepovers. High school was brutal as she watched friends pair up to date. One boy expressed interest in her, but she spent six months trying to hint that she wasn't interested before he finally gave up and moved on to another crush.

Amber began to struggle with depression at age 16 and had her first panic attack a month before graduation. Panic attacks became monthly events during the summer as pressure mounted to pick a career path and make long-term decisions about her life. Ultimately, she dropped out of community college after one semester due to weekly panic attacks and took an entry-level retail position.

Eric dealt with intense anxiety symptoms whenever the stability of any relationship came into question. This happened whether or not there was an actual problem, as Eric defined stability to mean the other person needed him. His early teen years were relatively uneventful, though he stayed away from dating due to extreme shame when he thought about potential sexual interaction.

When he reached high school, he continued to shy away from romantic partners. He got excellent grades and went to a prestigious college to earn his mother's approval. He had many friends from high school but none who really knew him well. He keeps in contact with them, though they know precious little about his emotional turmoil.

As the years passed and he became a teenager, **Chris** fell into depression. At age 16 his parents finally noticed his perpetually flat expression and took him to a doctor, who prescribed anti-depressants. Chris took these for a year before discarding them because "they still don't make me feel happy."

By the time Chris reached dating age he was starving for affection and latched onto the most damaged girl at his school who verbally and psychologically abused him. When she cheated on him, Chris rationalized her behavior as his own fault and worked harder to earn her approval. Despite being raised with some half-hearted Christian values, Chris used sexual prowess to please his girlfriend in a bid to keep her attention, but she continued to cheat on him. Suicidal feelings began to grow as he despaired of ever earning her faithful love. Finally, Chris found another damaged young woman who recognized his enabling behavior and beckoned him into her life to fulfill her needs instead. Chris only found the courage to leave his first girlfriend because he believed he could earn love more reliably elsewhere. He married this girl and had several children with her in their late teens and early twenties.

Ashley's sexual trauma showed her a clear way to earn approval from men and get people to keep her around. By junior high school, she was using sexual availability to get the boys at school to like her and she reveled in the belonging she felt. But using her body to earn approval while people disregarded her as a person left her feeling worthless to the few people she cared about. She began to believe she had no value as a human being apart from pleasing others with service, and her ability to service others sexually began to diminish as mental health symptoms increased. To this day, Ashley has never experienced an orgasm, but she fakes one every time.

Panic attacks began to set in whenever she tried to have sex, along with flashbacks to times of childhood abuse, but she kept these issues secret. The only outward signs of her internal turmoil were a begrudging resistance to intimacy and an expressionless, unenthusiastic performance during sexual activity. Her partners started to complain that she "wasn't fun anymore," and Ashley fell into despair as her only means of earning approval slipped away. Depression crashed into her life and caused her to plummet to the depths of misery.

THE DANCE OF ETERNAL DISAPPOINTMENT IN ADULTHOOD

Detachment issues, specifically the obsession with fluff over framework and the denial of needs leading to simmering resentment, find their climax in adult life, particularly in work, friendship, family, and marriage.

Work challenges insecure individuals on a daily basis. Their performance is literally measured and supervised to insure they're providing value to the company. Insecure individuals at work tend to constantly worry about perfection, though they secretly believe they'll eventually fail and be fired. Their first assumption about any surprise meeting is that they're about to be fired. Bosses tend to love them at first because they're so eager to please and never talk back.

As time wears on and their resentment toward management and coworkers builds, however, insecure individuals can be challenging to work with. They make a single mistake and are convinced they must now quit their job, so they compound the issue by calling out sick two or three days in a row after the small mistake. They don't get a requested day off and they seethe about it, dropping passive-aggressive comments or finding little ways not to fulfill work obligations which will ever so slightly inconvenience the scheduling manager.

Even if work ethic remains high, the insecure individual is just generally difficult to get to know. They rarely become an integral part of the team because that much attention and closeness frightens them. While the rest of the team works hard at bonding and growing together, the insecure individual seems to sit just outside the circle, refusing to enter. One notable exception to this is high-functioning individuals who can step into a position where they can make people happy, such as working as a volunteer for a hobbyist convention.

Friendship is desperately craved and desperately feared. Insecure individuals long to open up and connect with their friends. The need for intimacy devours them inside, but they know fulfilling that need is impossible. Times when they do open up about problems are followed with horror as they frantically apologize for causing an inconvenience by "wasting your time." They get embarrassed at having opened up and instead withdraw from the relationship, leading to a confusing situation for healthy friends who don't understand why they're suddenly being pushed away.

Family is an enormous challenge for insecure individuals. Their family is usually the core reason they have insecurity in the first place, so resentment boils under the surface at nearly every interaction. They may have one or two family members they trust or feel close to but this remains limited and they keep their finger on the ejector seat button at all times. Insecure individuals are most likely to complain to others about the behavior of their family members, especially parents or siblings they believe are more favored than they are. Inside, however, insecure individuals long to be accepted and loved by their family members, and they rarely walk away from even the most abusive of family systems.

Insecure parents tend to swap between two modes with their children: Best friend or tyrant. They start out worrying their children will hate them, so they attempt to please their children with gifts and money. These unasked-for gifts make the children happy in the short term, but they're usually left feeling unfulfilled and a little resentful as time goes on. The insecure parent doesn't understand this resentment and they react with hurt. They've paid for everything and sacrificed for their children, so insecure parents unconsciously believe they have the right to demand love and intimacy from their children. In fact, their children are usually the only people in the world they feel comfortable confronting or controlling. The price has been paid, and insecure parents tend to demand their children spend their entire lives paying them back at a moment's notice with attention and unquestioning obedience.

The flipside to this is when the children develop leverage such as controlling access to grandchildren and then push back. This causes the insecure parent to fear abandonment, whereupon they often collapse into approval-seeking behavior once more.

Marriage or long-term cohabitation is perhaps the most tumultuous relationship for insecure individuals. Two partners, at least one of whom has detachment behaviors, now have to build a life together, find meaning together, and make personal, individual decisions as a unified team. The couple may be in financial ruins due to the detached partner never saying "no" to user friends and family outside of the marriage. Children may be out of control with no boundaries or discipline because the detached parent seeks approval from them also. Even if these two areas are fine, the couple is often struggling under the surface, presenting a happy face to the world while sniping at each other behind closed doors the moment they don't have an audience for whom to perform.

Generally speaking, in their close relationships insecure individuals experience "episodes" where stress builds, needs go unmet, and there is a "blow up" with the friend, partner, or family member where they have to "talk it out" and "make up." As the other person is routinely punished for guessing needs wrong or missing secret signals which only make sense in hindsight delivered during screaming "episodes," confusion turns to anger. Relationships end without either side having a definite reason the relationship fell apart.

It's also common for insecure individuals to marry another person with similar insecurities and detachment, because entering into a permanent relationship based on this symbiotic dynamic seems the ideal solution to many detached persons. Neither partner wants to get too close, so neither partner ever feels challenged or worried about their own secrets being exposed. Even if one partner enters the marriage with healthy attachment behaviors, the marriage is likely to end up with two wounded and resentful people struggling to connect and meet their own needs.

What is left is two unhealthy communicators who struggle to state what they want or need, who expect their partner to understand instinctively how to help them, and who create secretive negotiations based on works and perceived debts. When the couple has children, it often marks a shift in the female partner from focus on her own self-worth to continuous obsession with the children's wellbeing as a means to earn approval and be "a good mother," which in turn leads her to mature herself in *some key areas,* though not all. She may pressure her detached husband to change his behaviors and "become a better father," but because he does not experience the emotional urgency in the same way she does, he typically responds by trying harder to meet her other needs while staying detached and anxious in the fatherhood role. He may even lash out at the children as they fail to live up to his emotional expectations or become sources of stress which his wife berates him over.

Resentment builds through the years until the couple has been married for fifteen years, has three children, and the wife wants out because her husband "makes the children feel so uncomfortable."

This whole mess tends to pass the detachment issues down to the children as well, creating a new generation of detached individuals.

Is modern society starting to make sense in a scary way?

At the core here is the issue of an "individuals together" versus a "unified partnership" mentality. The detachment issues make it almost impossible to connect and form a unified partnership, so the couple become individuals living together and making life choices in conflicting ways which threaten to tear their partnership in half.

One key thing to remember is this: In all their relationships, the insecure individual is acting out of love. As their love for a person grows and as the relationship deepens, their fear increases. The worst relationship in their life is so awful precisely because they love the person so desperately.

Some insecure individuals respond to all this pressure by checking out of relationships almost entirely. They spend their days and nights working, consuming entertainment media, and sitting alone in their bedroom. They may have one or two outlets for human interaction but by and large they keep themselves isolated. They frequently rationalize this isolation by saying,

"I'm just an introvert," and become defensive when this explanation is challenged.

The detached person who does choose to connect to others often says, "I am utterly miserable in every way, but I would rather die than lose this person. I love them so much that I'm willing to live in complete misery for the rest of my life rather than live without them." This is an obsessive love born of despair and hopelessness paired with a starving to belong and be accepted.

In cases of abusive friends, the insecure individual may be afraid that life will grow worse without the person. "What else will I have in my life?" is a common question when people ask why they don't end the friendship. Or they may fear that halting the abusive relationship will cause the other person to travel around to mutual friends and destroy each relationship the insecure person relies on, leaving them utterly alone. They're not at all confident in their ability to win such a struggle.

The insecure individual becomes stuck in an eternal cycle. They don't really believe there's any other way for them to behave and they begin to see their behavior as a natural response to the choices of those around them. The detached person fails to see their own behavior began with a flawed supposition about their own worth, or that they continue in their awful relationship patterns because they don't believe honest intimacy can truly exist.

Opening up emotionally, exposing oneself and being vulnerable, means risking everyone in their life finally seeing that secret thing inside of the detached person which caused their own family to abandon or reject them. That would be surrender. Worse, that would be suicide for all their relationships.

"There is no other way I can live," the detached person says. "This is the only path."

"Change is impossible because there's nothing for me to change to."

A LOOK AT OUR INDIVIDUALS

Amber has virtually no real friends. She has a host of online acquaintances who know just enough about her for her to call them friends, but she's ready to end any of the relationships at a moment's notice if they look like the person may want to meet in real life. She's tried online dating and it felt more manageable, but the partners always want to meet, which is a deal breaker for her. Amber spends her nights streaming anime and chatting with friends while flopped in her bed. She sees her family only on holidays when her mother guilts her into attending.

Eric spends most evenings with his friends playing tabletop games and card games. He says he has zero interest in ever dating. He works as a manager at the local animal shelter and makes good money which he invests in figurines of female characters he admires, which he calls "waifus". His entire apartment is filled with curio cabinets displaying thousands of dollars in scantily-clad figurines, fantasy swords, and cosplay gear. Eric struggles in his friend groups because he's never sure what anyone thinks of him. He's had to switch gaming groups a couple of times because of minor disagreements which he believed marked the end of the relationships, though he never actually confirmed the other parties didn't want him around.

Chris has been married to the same emotionally manipulative woman since high school. She says that Chris "never keeps his word" and is constantly violating her expectations. She complains Chris "ignores" their children and "doesn't spend enough time with them." Even when Chris does spend time with the children, his wife says he "yells at the kids" and "makes them feel worthless." She has complained about these behaviors for years and Chris admits to every fault she finds, promising to behave differently. The rare time he's tried to confront her about her hurtful behaviors or set boundaries, his wife claims he is "emotionally abusive" and "a narcissistic sociopath," a diagnosis which she got from watching television. His wife has had two online affairs where Chris has discovered her sending naked pictures to men she met on dating websites, but Chris says he's committed to maintaining the marriage and earning his wife's love.

Ashley has been divorced twice and has four children from four different men. She says she has no faith in marriage anymore so she's not going to get married again. She's currently with a boyfriend who is not the father to any of her children. He's been pressuring her to tie the knot and she says she enjoys the attention but doesn't trust him. She has only two female friends and describes them both as "drama mamas," and when she explains why, her descriptions of them match her own behavior patterns. Her friends are mostly male and mostly ex-boyfriends with whom she's had sexual relations. In fact, since entering adulthood, she's never managed to let go of even a single sexual partner, no matter how abusive. They keep coming back and she's always ready to complain to them about her current partner.

We've defined the problem. Now let's look at several ways an insecure person can slay their fear, shatter their emotional prison, and break through to a life of meaning.

CHAPTER 3
Fixing It with Self-Respect

DO YOU RESPECT YOURSELF?

Many people who suffer from severe insecurity flinch away from this question. They genuinely try to think about it, but their self-loathing is so intense their mind stops them from focusing on the answer. "What good could come from answering?" the brain asks. "You'll only get more depressed."

This is an important question to answer if a person is going to have any hope of changing. If you don't respect yourself, how can other people respect you? If you're a person you don't respect, how can you ever be satisfied? If you don't know whether or not you respect yourself, how can you know what needs to change?

A useful workaround for people who struggle with such a question is to externalize yourself as a separate person.

Imagine you have a friend exactly like you in every way. Same clothes, same hairstyle, same face, same body, same behaviors, same habits, same choices, same family. Same everything. They are absolutely exacting in replication. This is you, but it's someone else. Pick a different name for your externalized self, perhaps Jack or Jane.

Look at your friend. Inspect their behaviors and habits. Look at their choices. Answer the following questions:

1. Do you respect your friend?
2. Are they a person you look up to and want to be like?
3. Do their behaviors annoy you?
4. Do you feel your lip curling in disgust as you look at the way they allow themselves to be treated?
5. Are you angry at them for tolerating abuse?
6. Are you upset at them for telling foolish lies instead of speaking their mind?
7. Does your heart break for them at how they believe they're trapped but won't take a step forward because they believe there's no hope?

Look at your friend. Assess them closely.

Now imagine your friend is asking you for advice. They want to be happier. They want to feel safe and loved and fulfilled. They don't want to be abused and mistreated and walked all over anymore.

They want to become someone you respect. Not your approval, but your genuine respect.

They're asking you what they need to change about themselves to earn your respect.

What do you tell them? What things about Jack or Jane need to change to earn your respect? I encourage you to write this list down. Use bullet points if you want to be quick, but write out what your friend needs to change to earn your respect.

Maybe they should:

- Speak up more when they don't like what's happening
- Push back against manipulators and abusers
- Ask for what they want so they get their needs met
- Stop making small doubts into huge issues
- Finish creative projects instead of abandoning them halfway for not being perfect
- Put their creative works on display instead of hiding them in the dark
- Say "no" when they mean no instead of saying "maybe"
- Pursue what they want instead of letting other people take everything
- Stop taking misunderstandings personally
- Stop preemptively running away from relationships when they're afraid they might lose the other person

- Start living their life instead of just surviving emotional crises

Your advice to your friend is your roadmap for what you want to change about yourself. You've just created a plan to get your life on track and find satisfaction in the life you're living.

At this point, the fear sets in again. "This is a massive list with so many huge problems. It's impossible to fix all of these things today! Now that I know how unhappy I am, it's even worse than before!"

Stop, and take a breath. Remember to externalize.

How much of this list would your friend have to complete before they earned your respect? Is it enough to say, "Enough is enough, I am going to change"? How about when they take their first concrete step?

Most people respect another person the moment they stand up from the mud and take that first step into cleaning up their life. It takes a declaration of intent and then one solid action, and they earn instant respect. Every additional step earns new levels of respect. By the time they've completed the entire list, the people around them have mountains of respect for them, built carefully day by day as the person advanced toward fulfillment.

You don't have to be perfect to be worthy of respect. You just need to be taking action toward your goal. The more actions you take, the more respect you earn.

But how do you do this? If you knew how to accomplish all the changes on your list, you'd have done them by now.

Other people become necessary at this point. Look for people in your life, your social circles, or online who embody the changes you want to make in your life. Next to each list item you want to change about your behavior write the name of a few people you know or have heard of who embody the spirit of this new behavior. These can be people you know personally, historic characters of virtue, even action movie heroes. Whoever best embodies your change, write their name down.

Observe these people. Watch how they work and how they perceive problems differently from you. Read their books. Write to them and express an interest in becoming more like them. Ask for advice.

So many people fail to get help because they think no one will have time for them, but the vast majority of people who've worked hard to be where they are will be more than happy to help others achieve the same success. Most of them remember what it's like to feel so down and want to improve. The reason they're successful now is usually because they were so unsuccessful before and felt the drive to be better.

Reach out and find yourself a mentor. In your family, or in your church, at school, in a professional organization, wherever you find people you respect who embody one of the steps you need to take. Find someone with a life you want to live and ask them to teach you. Find a mentor online, read their book, and email them.

Therapists are useful as paid mentors for people who can't find someone in their own life or are too nervous to reach out and build an intimate relationship. Sometimes the professional relationship creates a buffer which enables the anxious person to take those first steps without fear of being rejected.

You are unlikely to change on your own. If you knew the answers, you'd likely have applied them by now. Reach out and find a mentor and a whole network of people like yourself. Make connections and effect the changes you listed.

Become a person you respect. If you don't respect yourself, no one else will.

A LOOK AT OUR INDIVIDUALS

Amber named her externalized-self Sarah. She decided Sarah would earn her respect best by finishing and publishing her fantasy novels. She found a group of indie authors online and worked with them to learn about publishing her own stories online. After some deep soul searching, she submitted her work to an indie author she met who had some success of their own and had opened an editing service. After getting the feedback, Amber worked on fixing up her manuscript until her editor friend told her it was ready to publish. She found an illustrator to draw up a cover and submitted her work to an online book publishing company. The feeling of sending her work out into the world was terrifying, but Amber respected herself for the first time in her life.

Eric examined his externalized self and decided his identical friend was unworthy of respect specifically because he let others push him around, especially abusive and manipulative female coworkers. Eric reached out to professional leadership groups for training on dealing with uncooperative employees. At those meetings, Eric made contact with several other managers in other fields who struggled with insecurity. They formed a small support group and held each other accountable for "doormat moments" with unruly employees. Finally, Eric confronted his manipulative female team lead at work on one of her unacceptable behaviors. She reacted with anger, and Eric ended up writing her up for her behavior. After the write-up, his employee seethed with resentment but changed her behavior. Eric was enormously proud to share the triumph with his accountability group.

Chris named his externalized self Max. Max, he realized, had no spine when it came to women. In fact, Max sought out the most damaged women he could and made himself a slave to their approval, then wondered why he was so miserable. Chris spent a week raging at Max in his head before he finally accepted that he hated himself. Chris reached out to male friends who had struggled in their marriages, both those who were still married and those who had ultimately divorced. These men assured Chris he had other options and did not have to live with his wife's emotional abuse. Armed with his friends' support, Chris stood up to his wife and for the first time refused to back down. After several challenging conversations, his wife threatened him with divorce. When Chris called her bluff and accepted her offer, she panicked. Her communications with Chris have shifted drastically to a place of mutual problem solving instead of blame. Chris is still not sure if he wants to stay in the marriage but he has earned his wife's respect, and his own.

Ashley didn't have to pick a name for her externalized self because she recognized that her two female friends are basically the same as she is, with the same damaging behaviors. This realization caused Ashley to plunge into depression for two weeks, but she eventually decided to do something about it. Her list of changes included an expectation to stop avoiding therapy. Ashley searched online and found an EMDR therapist in her area to help her manage the childhood sexual trauma which haunted her. Anxiety was high but she resisted the urge to cancel the appointment and had an intake with her new therapist. After her first session, Ashley felt hopeful about her chance to be happy for the first time in a decade.

CHAPTER 4
Fixing It by Investing in People

There's an insidious trap waiting for insecure people. The trap is a self-sustaining circle of cause and effect which leads the victim into a spiral of worry and disappointment.

This trap is called investing in outcomes.

The person with insecurity invests in outcomes by setting conditions for satisfaction based on certain events taking place. Investing in outcomes means you spend more time worrying about how people feel about you rather than the quality of those relationships. Outcomes are quantitative goals the person uses to mark an acceptable level of success. This happens when a person sets their measurement of success on getting a specific letter grade, or getting the highest grade in the class. The issue here is not just that they hoped to hit that mark, but that by reaching a successful outcome they believe they will **become worthy of love**. Or, more accurately, that they won't be found to be unworthy, today, at this time, in regards to this one thing.

Therein lies a second trap. The insecure person is never really proud of their accomplishments because each accomplishment is just an attempt to stave off abandonment and ostracization for one more minute. Accomplishments aren't stepping stones to a better life, the fruit of hard work, or worthy of praise. Praise makes an insecure person feel uncomfortable because it means the people praising them will expect consistent levels of accomplishment from now on, forever, and the insecure person believes they're really a failure. Praise means the stakes are higher, and the insecure person begins to panic under the pressure of perceived demands to be perfect.

Investing in outcomes also means that failing to hit arbitrary measurements of success means the insecure person believes they are worth even less than before. Now they're a loser, and everyone knows it.

Amber got a C on the midterm. She studied for two weeks in advance of the test, every single day for hours. She turned down fun with friends, locked herself in her room, and studied obsessively. She barely slept and ate only sparingly on sugary junk food. The day the test arrived she was so exhausted she could hardly think straight.

But now there's a C on her record. The teacher posted the results outside his office using student numbers instead of names. Amber is sure the other students somehow know her number. They file past the board and see that C and think, "Oh, that's probably the mousy looking girl who sits in the front row. How pathetic." Worse, she disappointed the professor. How can she stand to sit in class and have the professor look at her with such pity? Or even worse, what if the professor is mad at her? Having such a low grade will make the professor think she's not paying attention. She tries hard to look interested and nod and write things down every time the professor glances at her, but now he'll think it's all been a lie!

Amber's overall grade in the class is a high B, but after getting that C she's preparing to drop the class.

People invested in outcomes fear confrontation. Even the mildest disagreement with a friend can send them into a panic. Because of attachment concerns, abandonment can come from even mild disagreement, which boils into resentment, which turns into a complete lack of respect or love. Eventually their friend will hate them because they asked to go to a different restaurant! Instead of stating how they feel, the insecure person stays quiet and endures things they dislike, rude behavior, and unmet needs because to them the alternative is total loss of love. The outcome they need is for everyone to be happy with them and like them all the time, always, forever.

Parents who focus on outcomes set rigid goals for their children and punish them when they fail to meet these performance expectations. This is not the same as disciplining a child who comes home with an F for not doing homework. Instead, this is the parent whose child comes home excited and happy because they got a B on a very hard test but the parent says, "Next time, get an A." No praise, no acknowledgement, just a dismissal of effort and an expressed lack of worth. This crushes the child's self-esteem and leads to a rift between parent and child.

Partners who invest in outcomes take their significant other on a date. If the slightest thing is wrong, the insecure partner panics and apologizes. They spend the whole night trying to make up for the perceived disappointment. Or if their partner is worn out from a long day, the insecure partner takes it personally and feels like a failure. They invested in having the perfect night out and overwhelming their partner with euphoric bliss. Because these specific markers didn't happen, the date is now considered an utter failure. The couple may even have an argument over the perceived failure to hit the markers or show adequate appreciation.

So what does it mean to invest in people instead of outcomes?

The markers of success are the key difference. A person investing in people sets the mark of success at the best possible outcome for each party. This means they approach every situation saying, "I will make sure each person gets the most out of this that they can, given the circumstances."

In practice, this looks similar on the surface to investing in outcomes but the spirit is vastly different.

A person may get a C on the midterm after studying. They're disappointed, but they recognize they did the best they could under the circumstances. They may approach the teacher and express that they really thought they knew the material and ask for suggestions on what chapters to review. They look forward to the next test as an opportunity to show their growth, and they also recognize that they can pass the class just fine without the highest possible grade. They're invested in really learning the material and not in acquiring an arbitrary letter in the grade book.

Investing in people means confrontations become necessary. It's not loving to let a friend use heroin without saying something about your concern for their wellbeing. A person is not looking out for a sibling relationship when they let festering resentment build up for two years without saying something. The person invested in people confronts others with the goal of providing the best possible outcome for both individuals.

They push others to do better than their current behavior and help them understand why it's important to change. They give others a chance to improve themselves because the goal is to give that person a chance to be better, not to keep them around forever despite severe problems.

They invest in themselves as much as they invest in the other person and recognize they shouldn't be beaten down and ignored.

The person invested in people confronts others because that's the best possible chance for growth. They recognize the confrontation could be taken badly and lead to a relationship fracture, but they accept that risk because their goal is for both individuals to be as healthy and satisfied in life as possible. Even if the person gets angry and leaves them, the seed they planted today may sprout in ten years and lead to a much healthier friend down the line.

A parent may hope their child is the smartest in the class, but they accept honest effort. The goal is that the child learns the material and retains a natural curiosity and hunger for knowledge. Getting a B is good enough, though a gentle discussion about what topics were not fully clear could be helpful. Validating the effort is important and cannot be done if the parent is personally disappointed by the outcome. If the child gets a D, the parent doesn't take it personally and doesn't freak out at the kid. Instead, they sit down and make it clear the child is capable of much better than a D grade, and together they figure out what the most challenging obstacles were.

A partner invested in people instead of outcomes looks entirely different on a date. Something goes slightly wrong, but they laugh it off and quickly adapt with a new suggestion. Their significant other may be tired and yawning, so instead of taking it personally they suggest loading up on caffeine, going somewhere with more engaging activities, or even cutting the date short and heading home for a quiet movie night and an early bedtime. They don't take circumstances or lack of enthusiasm personally because the goal isn't to have a perfect night or push their partner to mindless ecstasy. The goal was to have the best possible time together, however that looks due to evolving circumstances.

The key difference is one of preserving versus growing. The person invested in outcomes is looking to preserve what they have and fears losing everything if outcomes aren't met. The person invested in people is looking to help themselves and others grow into the best life possible.

So how do you implement this in your own behavior?

If someone behaves inappropriately, don't get angry. Explain the inappropriateness to them. Either they take the lesson and your relationship gets better or they get mad and leave but carry the lesson with them.

If your financial outcome isn't what you wanted it to be, don't take it personally. Adapt. Find a new direction. Take the lesson and recognize failure doesn't mark your worth as a person, but it does provide a roadmap for where to grow.

Having a general plan for guiding your children is good. Micromanaging their decisions so they never grow beyond your control is smothering and will lead to either a weak adult or resentful estrangement. Educate your children for their own path.

Invest in yourself just as much as you invest in others. Without improving yourself and growing, you cannot hope to offer better love to others down the line. If you collapse without your needs met, you cannot give love to others. You are a better sister, brother, mother, coworker, and friend when your needs are met and you feel loved and satisfied. If you fail to respect yourself or get your own needs met, you will become resentful and bitter and hurt the people you love.

One clear sign of investing in outcomes instead of people is anger. If you're angry about outcomes, you're not investing in people. You're investing in your own vision for how other people should act. This is a fool's proposition and leads to endless frustration.

Investing in outcomes means you take it personally when plans don't come to fruition, because your own worth as a person has been negatively affected.

You deserve less love because you didn't hit your designated target. A person investing in people may feel a little disappointment at failure, but it isn't crushing and doesn't evoke huge emotional responses. They pick up, learn, and move on.

Investing in people means you are constantly adapting your plans. Target outcomes flow and shift fluidly as circumstances become clear. Planning an elaborate date and having the best possible night with a spouse looks differently after you've learned they're tired and just want to wrap up in warm blankets. Investing in outcomes means frustration, but investing in people means you shrug and adapt.

Invest in people. Invest in yourself. Remain fluid with plans and don't take outcomes personally. Adapt to outcomes by reinvesting in new ways to reach success.

A LOOK AT OUR INDIVIDUALS

Amber realized investing in outcomes was causing her panic attacks at school. She assessed the knowledge she'd gained from her first semester and realized that, while her grades had been high, she retained almost no information from any of the classes. She made an agreement with herself to take another semester at community college and not look at any homework grades or test grades until the end of the semester, even if it meant she might fail. Instead, she would only allow herself to gauge her success in the class based on how well she retained the knowledge. She intentionally invested in herself. She had panic attacks for the first three weeks until she settled into a comfortable studying rhythm. At the end of the semester, Amber finished all of her classes with straight-A's. She also picked a major and decided on a career path based on where her academic passion was strongest: teaching history.

Eric realized he was investing in outcomes by making sure other people were always happy with him. This had prevented Eric from standing up to people who mistreated him, but it also prevented him from getting genuinely close with anyone and sharing things about himself they might not like. Eric decided to end his loneliness by opening up to his best friend about some of his own insecurities. His friend expressed shock to hear Eric worried every single day, and was even more surprised to hear that Eric believed his friend was only pretending to like him. Eric invested in both himself and in his friend and opened up about his struggles. This allowed them to resolve misunderstandings and develop a deeper trust. By investing in individuals instead of outcomes, Eric created a more intimate friendship.

Chris decided the outcome he'd invested in was making his children happy at any cost in order to avoid his wife's anger. Now his kids were spoiled and had no respect for him. Chris resolved to invest in his children and their future wellbeing as adults. He created a list of expected behaviors and chores along with a list of matched consequences if the children refused to follow expectations. At first, they rebelled against the chart. Because Chris had stood up to his wife previously, the two parents were able to work together and parent on a united front, applying consequences according to the behavior chart they hung on the living room wall. After just a month the children were earning privileges through chores and speaking more respectfully to both parents. Their grades improved at school, and Chris believes they are finally on the path to becoming responsible adults.

Ashley was upset to discover that her desired outcome she invested in was to never be without a man in her life, the same as her mother had always done. She realized her sense of self-worth came from having several men around who desired her sexually, and that her current casual boyfriend was also a man she didn't respect but who spent all his time complimenting and pampering her. Ashley decided the best way to invest in individuals instead of outcomes was to break up with her boyfriend and force herself to be single for one year. During that year, she set out a list of behaviors in herself she wanted to see changed in order to earn her own respect. By investing in individuals instead of outcomes, Ashley was able to build self-worth and confidence for the first time in her life.

CHAPTER 5
Fixing It by Stopping the Worry Cycle

Perhaps the worst part about insecurity is just how much time it eats up in your average day.

Worries attack your mind every moment you're not busy. Tossing and turning before falling asleep. Waking up in the middle of night to continue worrying. While brushing your teeth. While standing in line at the grocery store. In the middle of class when you should be paying attention to the lecture. While trying to read a book, so you have to read the same sentence ten times.

When the average person would be thinking about hobbies or looking forward to an enjoyable future date, the insecure individual is running preemptive damage control on things they either think they did wrong or believe they could do wrong in the future.

This worrying usually revolves around relationships, but some sources of anxiety might be surprising.

Did you know academic performance is tied to relationships? Think about it. When you're a little kid you're given grades you think indicate how smart you are. The grades get handed directly to your parents who may or may not approve of your efforts. The slightest challenge in your relationship with them can send that stress level skyrocketing. If you believe that you are only loved based on the work you do, the quality of your outcomes, that grade means everything.

It's not that insecure people worry about actually being the smartest person in the world; the problem is that they have to be as smart and successful as possible in order to overcome how truly unlovable they are.

This means that any social interaction or any activity at all can be cause for worry. Knowing that a social gathering like a party or family reunion is coming may send an insecure individual into a spiral of worry. They may struggle to sleep at night, maybe even for weeks on end in anticipation of the event. They're usually running over and over different scenarios in their head in case something goes wrong or they're asked something they don't expect. They rehearse answers to common questions, or they rehearse damage control propaganda so they can pretend to laugh off family stories about mistakes they made. They practice explaining how it was a complete misunderstanding, and they don't even think about that mistake at all anymore!

The goal is to make the damage control spins sound as convincing as possible because they need their audience to believe. Conversations are no longer a natural flow between people who care for each other, but instead take on the presentation of a performance. This constant performing is why insecure individuals also frequently do well with acting, role-playing games, improvisation comedy, and other creative pursuits which require them to pretend to be someone they are not. They're doing this all the time, after all.

At stake here is, as described in previous chapters, an obsession with outcomes. They are obsessed with the idea of maximizing their chance to reach the correct outcome in any scenario. They define ahead of time what that acceptable outcome will be, namely that they are fully accepted and their unlovable secret remains cloaked and hidden from the probing gaze of others.

Because they are invested in the outcome over the relationship, their social interactions tend to be superficial and defensive in nature, making it difficult for the other parties to really enjoy the time together. Other people may feel like the conversation is very one-sided. For some, this is no big deal, because they enjoy talking about themselves so much that the insecure individual becomes the "greatest listener in the world". But relationships don't thrive on only one person sharing themselves and being vulnerable and intimate. So, over time, it usually becomes apparent the insecure person is at best hesitant to speak about themselves and at worst is doing conversational gymnastics to dodge sharing their own opinions, thoughts, or principles.

Principles is really the core of the solution here. Investing in outcomes, as we discussed before, leads to frustration, misery, and disappointment. It also leads to resentment on both sides as the other party fails to live up to your hidden expectations. And when they feel shut out or feel like there is no purpose in speaking with you because there is no substance to conversations, they may grow resentful or distant as well.

So how do you invest in yourself? How do you invest in those around you?

It probably sounds like an insurmountable task. It sounds like I'm telling you to just go out there and start talking about how you feel and let everything out and never hold back ever again. This false dichotomy is part of the problem exactly. Insecure people only let it all out when they're angry, otherwise they bottle it all up inside to prevent accidentally sharing.

Principles are the answer. What an insecure person should do is select 3 to 5 core principles they believe are truly important in their life. Identify the principles of people you respect, or draw them from a religious setting such as the Bible, or even from action heroes in movies. These do not need to be principles that you are living perfectly every single day. In fact, you almost certainly won't be! It's likely that you've failed continuously to a uphold them. That's exactly the reason you have such constant self-loathing.

It is enormously difficult, indeed probably impossible, to respect yourself if you do not stay true to the principles you believe are most important. If you believe honest people are the best people and that only honest people can really be worthwhile but you are constantly lying and hiding and obscuring the truth, you will automatically believe that you are not a good person.

The problem is that your anxious brain is telling you the truth will get you killed, or at least abandoned and depressed enough to kill yourself. If you believe everyone in your life is going to abandon you completely and that you will die without their approval, it becomes way too hard to tell the truth. There's no benefit.

But what's worse? Having people hate you for the truth, or feeling completely empty inside and hating yourself? If you had your own respect for adhering to your principles but a few people rejected you for sticking to your principles, would you be better off or worse off than you are now?

This is a question of developing the anxiety forcing you to change so it overcomes the anxiety forcing you to resist change. Will you be more or less miserable in the long-term? Will your friends, family, loved ones? Who will suffer if you keep things as they are, and what might be the terrible cost years from now?

Something else to think about is this: if people will reject you standing for your principles, are they someone you really want in your life? Is their approval actually worth anything if they only approve of people who don't have principles?

Select 3 to 5 principles you believe are truly important and never want to violate. You will violate them, but the point is not to expect perfection from yourself. Never expect perfection, but pursue it relentlessly. These 3 to 5 principles will become your guiding decision-making markers.

How do these principles interrupt the worrying? Instead of tossing and turning all night, or rehearsing conversations in the shower, you simply dedicate yourself to living these principles and answering in ways that are best in line with them regardless of cost.

Let me show you how this works.

You decide that honesty is the best policy. You want to never lie again, even if it leads to misery and death. You decide you have to respect yourself even if it means no one else wants to be around you. Great! Except, at a family event, someone asks if you remember doing something embarrassing.

Boom, anxiety spiral.

The common response for insecure people is to deny the mistake ever happened or to convince the other person they are either remembering it wrong or that it was not as bad as they remember. But if unflinching honesty is your policy, you own the embarrassing mistake and then state how you have grown from it. You don't have to wallow in humiliation or make degrading comments about how stupid you are. You calmly recognize that you are not that person anymore, and you own the mistake.

If you saw someone do this, would you think they were completely stupid because of a mistake they made in the past, or would you be impressed by how calmly they handled the reminder? Would you respect them for owning their mistake? Would you be more for less likely to want to spend time with this person?

Let me give you another example.

You decide love is the most important quality a person can embody. You decide to be absolutely loving to the people around you at all times. This means you're going to do what's really best for them, and not what either of you may want. Instead of enabling a friend who's been living on your couch for six months and won't get a job, you decide to do what's really best for them and for you. You sit them down and have a conversation about how they've become too comfortable and it's not best for them to stay with you for free anymore. Maybe they have to pay rent, or maybe it's time to just get out.

Neither one of you is really happy and it's deadly to the friendship to continue this way. Sure, they might get mad at you, but this confrontation is really the most loving thing you can do for both of you. If you to let the behavior continue, it will make them miserable and lazy in the long-term. If you're going to love them, you need to have the hard conversation.

If someone had a hard conversation with you, would you be more or less likely to respect them? Even if it was something you didn't want to hear? If you saw someone else lay down a firm, loving boundary with a friend who was using them, would you be more likely or less likely to trust that person in the future? Do you respect people who enable other people instead of giving them hard truths? Or do you respect people who have clear boundaries?

There are many principles. Honesty. Love. Courage. Work ethic. Charity. Compassion. Perseverance. Loyalty. Pick 3 to 5 and dedicate yourself to living those principles from now on. When you find yourself tossing and turning at night, or find your mind spinning around on how to control the damage of an embarrassing truth or difficult confrontation, remind yourself that you are a person who lives to your principles. Tell yourself that when the situation arrives you will answer in a way that is really in line with your principles.

And then, do it!

When someone confronts you with a topic that bothers you, when you feel the growing anxiety, ask for a few seconds to think about it. Just say, "Let me think a second." Then think about your principles and how best to apply them.

Acknowledge the unprincipled things your anxiety wants you to do, and then ask yourself if you can live knowing you did that instead of sticking to your principles.

Think about later tonight when you're lying in bed miserable about how you don't respect yourself for having fallen through when you had a chance to live your principal.

Think about later on when you have to uphold this lie again and again and again and violate your principles every single time.

How many more times will this failure to hold to your principles come back to haunt you?

Is it better to get the pain over with right now?

And then, you explain your principle. You can begin your new approach by sharing with the other person how you're going to respond. You can acknowledge that you're nervous about telling them the truth, but you believe honesty is the best approach, so you're going to be completely honest with them. Yes, they may brace for impact on hearing this, but they'll listen closely.

By explaining your principles, you also demonstrate what your principles are so the other person can begin to know you and respect you. You portray yourself as a person of real principle, because you are! This is no longer acting and pretending.

Explain your principles to the person and then apply them. What kind of person would hate you for sticking to your principles? They may disagree with your application of the principle, and you can discuss that together, but don't let them sway you back into insecurity so that you violate your principles.

Manipulative people will try to convince you not to stick to your principles. Other principled people will say something like, "I can respect that." They may tell you they don't like it, but that does not mean you have to change your answer. You can even tell them you're sorry that it comes down to this, but you must stay firm with your principles. The people you want in your life will respect this and will want you around more because of it. They are more likely to find a peaceful solution with you because you have demonstrated you are a person of quality, it is very valuable to have people of quality in your life.

By finding 3 to 5 principles, pausing to think about decisions, applying your principles, explaining your principles, and sticking to them 100%, you will shift yourself from a person you don't really like into a person you do respect. You will also make yourself a person of real substance. Other people of principle will love you and want to be around you.

The truth is that insecure individuals think that by having no principles they will stop other people from objecting to them, and that this means they will be loved. In fact, it is almost impossible to love someone who has no principles, because they have no substance. How do you love a cardboard cutout? How do you love a cloud of fog?

Stop the cycle of worrying by changing the priorities which dictate your responses.

Discover your principles and begin living them.

A LOOK AT OUR INDIVIDUALS

Amber used to worry what she would do if she received a poor grade. At the start, she was having panic attacks as she worried about failure. This worrying often caused her to crumble and sabotage her own efforts. Instead, she resolved to hold Perseverance as her greatest principle, that she would continue working to improve herself no matter what problems she faced. After she published her first book she received several good reviews along with one or two critical comments. Instead of crumbling under the disapproval, she learned from the criticisms and used them to make her future works better. She powered through college and forced herself to learn everything she could about her chosen field without measuring her ability based on professors' test grades. She began racking up accomplishments, and each setback only served to show her where to focus her future improvements.

Eric took Honesty as his most important principle. When he was tempted to lie or hide the truth, Eric would instead say, "I hold honesty as the best policy no matter what, so in the interest of complete honesty, here's what I really think." People began responding to Eric with more respect as he told them the truth, and their own efforts improved due to his valuable insights which he'd held back before for fear of offending someone. People in his life started to regard Eric as a valuable advisor and consultant on their projects because he'd tell them where he saw mistakes, even if the mistake was their own unhealthy behavior.

Chris used to collapse into the goals others set in order to earn their approval. He resolved to make Courage his guiding principle. Whenever Chris felt fear, he targeted that reaction for immediate action. He forced himself again and again to face whatever made him most afraid. As he systematically faced each fear and overcame them, Chris' life was transformed from a wasteland of desperate avoidance to a fulfilling system of relationships and meaningful work which Chris himself valued. By living with total courage, Chris tore down his old life of fear and built a stronger family for his children to grow up in.

Ashley realized what she lacked most was Compassion. This became her guiding principle in her behaviors toward others. Where before she would lash out at people for having needs, instead she worked to help people feel fulfilled. Without enabling, Ashley was able to give warmth and kindness to the people in her life who were hurting. She stopped focusing on her own pleasure and on keeping available resources and instead used the resources she had to help others. As she did so, Ashley found a growing respect for herself and was finally able to call herself a good person. She discovered a love for helping others and shifted her perspective to one of service to others instead of keeping them around to use them. She volunteers now at a women's shelter and works to meet the needs of other women who've suffered sexual violence as she did.

CHAPTER 6
Fixing It by Finding your Purpose

Most people in modern society have no idea what the purpose of their life is. When you ask them to define the meaning of life, they give that vague, cliché answer about how no one really knows the meaning of life.

I'm here to tell you that answer is crap.

There is absolutely purpose in every human life. To find this purpose, though, you need to look beyond the modern materialistic focus. Our modern setting obsesses over the self. We are encouraged to focus on what we can own and gather and accumulate, how attractive we can become, how much sex we have. The emphasis is on the individual experience and accumulation, but this is utterly false. When a person dies, their experience dies with them.

A dead person after their funeral is not remembered for how much sex they had. The dead person's possessions are descended upon by everyone with a claim to the estate. Money is ripped apart and divvied up, while actual physical possessions are squabbled over or thrown away.

Consider the fact that everything you own will likely one day end up in a dumpster.

Sure, your kids may want to keep some sentimental souvenirs, but they'll likely stuff them in a box in their attic to be discovered upon their death when their children will then throw the souvenirs away without even realizing what they are.

Your money will be squandered away and disappear into bills and car payments or expensive cosmetic surgeries.

If you put stock in your video game accomplishments, no one will care how many achievements you unlocked the day after your funeral. They're not going to engrave your gaming profile on your headstone, after all. Same with the number of books. Who cares about any of that after your funeral?

So the grand question becomes: if none of these things matter, then what does? What survives beyond the day after your funeral? This is where we discover the purpose of life.

Consider the people you've lost. You remember them fondly, but why does their memory stick with you? What was important about them? The answer usually lies in the impact they had on your life. We treasure memories of people who helped us when we needed it most or mentored us when we didn't know what else to do. We hold up with honor and revere people who reach out to others and rescue them from darkness.

The impact a human being has on the lives of those around them is what survives beyond death and echoes into eternity.

When you start out alone, your decisions affect no one but yourself. A few responsibilities are all you face. Feeding yourself, occasionally washing your socks, and making sure you have enough money for pizza. When you get married, you share those decisions with another human being and are at least partly responsible for their well-being, insomuch as you don't negatively impact their quality of life. When you have children however, you also become responsible for their well-being. Your decisions take on a greater purpose and meaning because they will have lasting repercussions for your children.

Let's assume the right now you are a twentysomething hip single person living a great lifestyle. Nonstop parties and all the burritos you can eat. For the sake of this discussion, let's assume that:

- You get married and have 3 kids in the next 10 years.
- 30 years after that, your children will also get married and have 3 children.
- 30 years after that, your grandchildren will get married and have 3 children.
- 30 years after that, your great-grandchildren get married and have 3 children.

That means that 100 years from now, you will be looking at great-great-grandchildren. If we assume each of your children has three children, and each of their children has three children, and so on until that fifth generation, you will end up with **120 biological descendants** in the next 100 years. Including their spouses who are obviously directly impacted by their lives, you will have **240 descendants.**

This is **120 marriages** modeled on your marriage. These are **240 lives** directly impacted by the decisions you make on an everyday basis.

Is that enough pressure for you? Well then, here, have some guilt.

The bad decisions you make ripple downward through this branching tree of descendants. When you choose to be unhealthy, or when you foolishly spend money, you are risking this entire tree. Letting emotional wounds fester damages your legacy and diminishes your ability to create a healthy family tree over the next 100 years.

Feel that surge of anxiety, that burning urgency? Good. You should feel pressure every single day to provide the best possible outcome for all of your descendants, because as we have established, your impact on the human lives around you is what really matters.

So, ask yourself this: what do your spreading ripples look like so far?

Okay, I get it. Huge question, and probably not an encouraging answer.

The good news is that your bad decisions don't actually have to damage this tree. What really damages the tree of descendants is when you refuse to learn from those mistakes. As I'll show in a minute, your bad decisions can even be *helpful* in developing a healthy tree.

If you are the only person present on this entire tree, the point of your life is to minimize your pain and maximize your pleasure in a completely hedonistic, pleasure-soaked life until the day you die. Any mistake you make deprives yourself of potential pleasure and means that your life was less than perfect.

But when looking at this from a legacy view, mistakes actually can be quite valuable. That is, as long as you turn those mistakes into lessons you can teach to your descendants to strengthen them against making those mistakes themselves, or help them sort through mistakes they see others make. This transforms tragedies, missteps, and just generally bad things into useful data to strengthen your legacy.

And that's what this is all really about: a living legacy of human descendants whose lives are fundamentally transformed because you existed in this world. They may remember the story about how great-great-grandfather suffered a similar tragedy to themselves and draw strength from the family stories. Or, they may not remember you at all 500 years from now, but the family has simply learned the skills to overcome those issues because you taught them to the first few generations. Therefore, when they come up against the same problems they may not remember you at all, but the issues are no problem at all for them to deal with. Your memory may be gone, but your impact remains.

This is how we fundamentally transform the world around us. The only way to make change happen is to impact the lives of a significant number of people through our limited years to spread health and growth at an exponential level.

Now a lot of you reading this book are going to be saying something like, "But I don't want to have kids! This is useless to me."

This tree of descendants is not only true for biologicals. You may adopt, foster, or mentor a child, save someone's life, become a doctor and cure them of a crippling disease, become a lawyer and free them from an unjust accusation, or any other number of ways you could significantly impact a human life in such a way that you can fundamentally shift the trajectory of that life onto a better vector. A Catholic priest who will never marry and never have children may nonetheless have a larger tree of descendants and living legacy than a married father of five. It's all in the number of impacts.

In fact, the original estimate of three descendants from you is extraordinarily low. If I may use myself as a not-so-humble example, the average therapist may see **50 to 100** clients every year. If I work as a therapist for 40 years, that means a potential impact number of **4,000** clients. This does not include all my children, friends, other therapists I mentor, and people impacted by this very book in your hands. Anyone whose life I have fundamentally changed in my work to put them on a better course becomes a part of my living legacy. Hopefully, by the end of my life, I will have thousands or even tens of thousands of ripples directly from me. That increases again when you look at all the ripples those people will go on to create. Imagine if I have an initial impact of **4,000**, but 10 of those are therapists

I mentor who will have **4,000 impacts of their own**. That's **40,000 impacts** through those therapists that gets added to my initial **4,000.**

Just because of my line of work, I'm looking at a potential impact of **44,000 human lives** in the next 40 years. And none of those people are even related to me in any way.

Now that we've got the scope of your living legacy plotted out, let's talk about fractured legacies versus unified legacies. You must choose one of these to define your own legacy of descendants.

You can have a unified legacy where everyone works together in a healthy way with good skills, open communication, confidence, and the ability to keep that living tree going indefinitely until the end of time. Remember that your descendants and living legacy are not static creatures, but dynamic living beings who will go out and create ripples of their own. A unified legacy works toward healing the world around them and creating a better environment for all the children who come after. They may not even realize they are part of the same tree, but when two members of a unified legacy meet, their work is magnified by mutually shared intention.

Or, you can create a fractured legacy of broken people spiraling off into the dark, lacking in skills, and believing that they do not deserve to be loved. You can make the world a better place, or the worst place. Create a world of broken people who tear down the things of value in exchange for approval from people who don't respect them. Send forth dozens of descendants who only know how to scream in anger at each other, or who collapse at the slightest chance of confrontation. When two members of broken legacies meet, their mutual weakness creates a sucking void of misery which draws in innocent bystanders and makes life unbearable for their loved ones.

Many people think that they can hide away from the world and have no impact at all. This is extraordinarily difficult, as you will likely have interactions with at least one human being in your life. However, if you manage to have truly zero impact anyone, stay alive in your apartment by eating delivery pizza slipped under the door, doing online work only, and staying totally alone without any real human impact, your life will have meant nothing.

Actually, your life will have been nothing but masturbation.

There will be nothing which survives you, except a likely fragrant and filthy apartment that someone else will need to empty out and occupy.

If you live a life completely devoid of impact, your life has been nothing but masturbation. But living a life which detracts from your living legacy and fractures it is worse than masturbatory. Damaging your own legacy means that it would have been better for you not to have ever lived at all. At that point, the best possibility is that people in the future will eventually overcome your bad memory and erase your existence entirely. You will not be worthy of memory and they will simply move on as if you never lived. Your life would then return to meaning nothing.

Now, this legacy focus does not mean you can neglect other areas of life. Indeed, with this perspective, everything becomes about your legacy. Eating healthy, attending to your finances in a responsible way, selecting careful romantic partners in case of accidental reproduction, and building a stable home to insure maximum emotional health for your children are all enormously important for your living legacy. Working on your mental health becomes vital as you can hand down those lessons you've learned. Mistakes you make are also valuable, as we discussed previously.

500 years from now when you and I are dead and dust and no one even remembers that we lived, the impacts that we had on the lives of those around us and the way those impacts fundamentally altered their lives will survive. This is because the impacts don't stop, but rather travel onward as each of those people impact other lives. This is an infinite chain of impacts with improved lives and better living conditions, and a frankly better world, which survives you. The world is better and different because of the small initial impact you make.

Do not be afraid to engage with other people. This in fact is the only thing that makes life worthwhile. The purpose of your life is to change the world in positive ways so that those who live 500 years from now, whether they remember your name or not, will be better off because you live now.

Your life absolutely has meaning. Your life absolutely has purpose. Your life absolutely has hope, because no matter what happens, you can hand a valuable lesson to future people who will need it desperately.

Start living your life in a way conducive the living legacy you want to leave. Think about the day after your funeral, and build for it.

The time is now, and you can do this.

One final thought: make sure your legacy can live just fine without you. If those in your family are entirely dependent upon you for good decision-making, finances, and to play peacemaker, what happens to them if you die? Building a good legacy means building a self-sustaining legacy that can survive the death of one or two powerful individuals.

Feel that pressure yet? Good. Use it to create urgency.

Now get out there and start building that living legacy.

CHAPTER 7
Fixing It by Developing Emotional Intimacy

YOU MUST UNLEARN FALSEHOODS

Insecurity in relationships is an issue of perspective.

The detached individual's view of the world and their place in it is skewed because they carry a fundamental misunderstanding about relationships and love. The old equations from childhood are still logged in the back of their head and intercepting all decisions before their rational adult mind can even process them.

A few examples of what this looks like in practice:

Ashley texts her husband asking about dinner plans. After ten minutes, he still has not texted back. Ashley begins to wonder what he's found that's more important than she is. She sends texts again and again, growing more and more upset as the minutes tick by. Finally, convinced that her husband has abandoned her for another woman, she sends angry texts lashing out at him for not responding. A few minutes later she regrets her anger and sends texts begging him not to read the first texts and apologizing profusely if he already has. Two hours after asking about dinner plans, Ashley is an emotional wreck and believes the marriage is over.

As she's packing an overnight bag to leave before her husband can come home to scream at her and abandon her, her husband texts her back to say he's been in a work meeting the whole time.

Eric's friends are often busy with work and children. He's tried to spend time with one of his friends, Steve, several times, but Steve has five kids and has had to cancel plans at the last-minute multiple times, always citing trouble finding a babysitter or his kids being sick. After the first time Eric wondered if Steve was just avoiding him, but by the third time he's sure of it. Eric doesn't confront Steve about the concerns and always acts cheerful when they have to reschedule, but inside he's seething with disappointment and wonders why he's not good enough for Steve to spend time with. Eric stops taking Steve's phone calls and texts because he knows deep down that Steve never wanted to be friends with him in the first place and all these attempts to act friendly are just for show.

In both examples, the reader can no doubt see a clear breakdown of logic. If either of the individuals had stopped to ask for clarification on the opposite party's behaviors or intentions, the issue could be easily resolved. In fact, it's likely that the other party has no idea whatsoever of the calculations and desperation taking place in the detached person's mind until the emotional suffering spills over and creates a relationship catastrophe which seems like a life-or-death battle to the end.

But the insecure individual doesn't need to ask, because they already know. Their foundational equation says that all disappointments are personal, and all choices other people make are done either with complete disregard for the detached person or in an effort to exploit and hurt them. In the detached person's mind they are an object of scorn, pity, and resentment in the eyes of others, a burden to be borne and no more.

When I work with detached people, I conduct the following perspective exercise. This is usually done with the eyes closed to heighten the inner imagination, but the constraints of reading this material makes closing one's eyes pointless. Instead, the reader is strongly encouraged to thoroughly consider each of the following points before moving on to the next.

Imagine you are in a relationship with the perfect partner. Truly perfect in every way.

This partner tells you exactly what they want and expect up front. Not in a demanding way, but in a calm and simple manner, straightforward and completely honest. When they need something from you, they ask for it the moment they need it. Even if you can't provide what they need at that moment, they let you know the need is there up front and right away. Their expectations are clear and you know exactly what it takes to make them happy. You know the exact boundaries of the relationship and what would hurt them. You also know exactly what would cause them to sever the relationship.

When you do something they don't like, your perfect partner tells you right away on the very first time. They say something like, "Oh, I don't really like that, could you do this instead?" They don't wait until you've done the wrong thing several times, and they don't pretend to like it to be nice. They tell you immediately while no one is angry or embarrassed. Problems are fixed when they're tiny and are not allowed to grow any larger because they lay out a simple plan to fix the issue right away.

When you do something they like, they tell you and praise you for it. They also tell you exactly why they liked the behavior so you can understand their way of thinking and repeat their happiness with other gifts. You know exactly what they like up front so you can be certain they're pleased in the relationship.

You know at any time what the other person needs, what they don't like, and what they do like. You know how happy or unhappy they are without guessing, and they give you clear paths to fix whatever the issues are right away.

Reader, given a partner like this, answer the following questions:

Do you believe this partner trusts you?

If you are meeting their needs consistently, would you feel confident in yourself as a good partner?

With them telling you exactly what they do and don't like right away, would you feel secure in a marriage like this?

The majority of people would say that, yes, this partner trusts them. Needs are shared openly and right away. This perfect partner shares their dislikes openly without fear of being abandoned or rejected, they are trusting you to be reasonable and solve the issue without a fight. They are completely open without reservation.

Meeting your partner's needs is how people feel like a good partner. If a person knows exactly what to do, does it consistently, and is praised every time for it, they can feel confident that their partner values them and feels positively toward them. This person can hold up their head and be proud of caretaking their mate in the best possible way.

Knowing what the person doesn't like and being told on the spot that something went wrong is enormously important. Praise is hollow and empty if no negatives are ever mentioned. How can a person trust someone who never says what's wrong? However, knowing what a person dislikes and being confronted right away means nothing will ever boil under the surface, the guessing games stop, and praise can be trusted because the person is completely honest with their feelings.

Now, reader, consider carefully the following scenario.

You are with the most terrible partner you can imagine.

This partner does not tell you what they need or want, not in any clear way. A thousand small hints which make sense only to them are sprinkled throughout conversations. Sometimes you're able to decipher what they want, but most of the time you only find out you missed a clue when they're angry and snapping at you later for having "ignored" them. You don't know what they expect out of the relationship apart from some vague notion of "staying together" and "being happy." You have no idea what upsets them apart from missing their secret signals. You live in fear of accidentally stepping on a landmine and blowing up the relationship because you have no idea what would make them end the marriage.

This terrible partner doesn't tell you when you do something they dislike. At least, they don't tell you right away. Instead they pretend to like what you did, or they give vague grunts but don't respond otherwise. Several months will go by until they have a bad day and then they blow up, shouting at you about everything you've done wrong which they've held bottled up all this time. They play the victim, put-upon and miserable under your inconsiderate care. This cycle repeats itself over and over as you try to correct mistakes, but for every issue you fix a new one arises which you won't find out about until the next storm.

When you do something they like, they don't really tell you. They may say thank you but mostly they act embarrassed or dismissive. You never really know what makes them happy because sometimes the same gift will elicit opposite reactions, upsetting them and kicking off another shouting match. Mostly your gifts and kind acts go unanswered and unacknowledged.

Reader, given a partner like this, answer the following questions:

Do you believe this partner trusts you?

If you never know what their needs are but are told you consistently fail to meet them, would you feel confident in yourself as a good partner?

With no idea when you might step on a landmine and end the relationship by accident, and with them bottling up their unhappiness until they're enraged enough to shout at you and hurt you for the perceived insults, would you feel secure in a marriage like this?

The answer to all three questions is a resounding, "No!"

The lack of honesty and openness creates intense distrust and speaks volumes about the partner's refusal to trust anyone.

Refusing to share needs with a partner means that partner will forever lack confidence and feel like a failure in their own marriage.

The above exercise is not limited to romantic relationships, either. Replace "partner" with "friend" and all of the points hold true. Friendship flourishes with trust and openness. Resentment and secrecy destroy friendship.

Secretiveness about disappointments and refusing to correct misunderstandings means resentment will boil until the person finds a reason to end the relationship or finds a new friend to replace the current one. Neither party can feel secure in this relationship because it is one argument away from complete destruction.

Even worse, pretending things are fine while seething with resentment poisons even the genuinely good times the friends may share. Every few months the detached friend explodes and says that "everything" has been wrong and they've been "so unhappy this whole time." The other friend hears this and believes even the good times were fake and pretend. In the future, any moments of happiness become suspected of being lies. Joy turns to doubt and the friends cease to enjoy time together, because who knows when it will be revealed that every smile was pretend?

To the detached persons reading this book: Recognize that you have been the terrible friend. Through your fear and obsessive love you have robbed your loved ones of the ability to feel trusted, to feel confident, or to feel secure. Your loved ones live in perpetual uncertainty and fear because of the doubt and distrust you have seeded throughout relationships with your refusal to engage.

That's the bad news. Most detached clients hear that and hang their heads in shame. There's a certain horror at being the person who wounds others, especially those who are most loved and valued.

Now for the good news:

Sharing needs is not the burden detached people have been led to believe. In fact, as the above exercise shows, sharing needs is an incredible gift to the other party. Sharing disappointments creates an opportunity to build trust and deepen understanding with one another. Communicating about the things which please us means we get more of them, and the person giving them can feel confident in their own good work.

Sharing our needs is one way we take care of our loved ones and help them to be fulfilled.

DON'T MAKE ME BEG

At this point in the discussion, most detached individuals feel a surge of anxiety and hopelessness. To sum up:

- What you've been doing has been hurtful to your loved ones
- You now realize you are a serious problem in your relationships
- Your behavior must change because continuing this way makes you feel like a bad person
- The only way to fix your relationships is to do the most terrifying thing you can imagine
- You still face an internal belief which says openness is hopeless and will definitely cause abandonment no matter what some jerk therapist may tell you

To acknowledge this internal struggle, I usually say something like, "But asking for your needs sounds like it would be begging, right? 'Please please please give me what I want'?"

The detached client nods at me. "Yeah, that's how it feels."

So the answer is to create a system where openness and honesty do not feel like begging.

ENTER THE EXPLICIT SHARING OF NEEDS

Needs must be stated explicitly in order to be met.

Go back to the framework idea once again: There exists in every relationship a negotiation table. Piled on each side are the needs and expectations each person holds for the relationship. Now that we acknowledge endless fluffing will never save a relationship, the only recourse is to sit down at the negotiation table and hammer out a trade.

Most detached individuals start with indirect attempts to share. They spring ideas on their loved ones at the last second and mask the needs as casual whims.

Instead of calmly stating, "I really feel disconnected from you lately because we haven't had much time together," the detached person says, "Hey, how about we get some dinner and watch a movie tonight at seven o'clock?"

Their spouse, not knowing this is about an unmet need, looks surprised and says, "Oh, sorry, I have plans with my friends tonight." The spouse walks away feeling pleased because their partner wanted to spend time together. "How nice," they think with a smile.

But the detached partner is crushed. "How could they reject me like that? They don't want to spend time with me? What could be more important than our marriage?" Resentment builds, and the unsuspecting spouse has no idea what just happened.

Instead, there is a simple way of communicating these explicit needs openly. I say "simple" and not "easy" because this level of openness will cause flutters of immense anxiety in the detached person.

THE NEW SKILL

Hold out your left hand palm upward and say, "I really need _____" and fill in the blank with your need. This may sound like any of the following:

- "I've been feeling lonely and need to spend quality time with you."
- "It's been several days since we had sex and I need us to have some fun."
- "I feel cooped up in the house and need to get out for a while."
- "I feel stressed taking care of the kids and need you to take over for an hour or two while I cool off."
- "I need some time with my friends."
- "I need some time alone to recharge."
- "I need you to stop shouting at me."
- "I need you to stop accusing me of deception."
- "I need you to start asking for clarity before you react to your assumptions."

Sharing these needs makes us feel vulnerable. Exposed. Naked. Being so open reveals who we are, what we need, and our values as a person. The detached person is risking exposing that secret thing down inside of them which causes them to be so unlovable. The fear spikes as they're about to open their mouth, and their throat closes. They feel like they're begging and creating a burden on their loved one. They fear the only outcome will be abandonment or begrudging resentment.

A second communication skill is needed.

ENTER THE NEGOTIATION STAGE

You've just stated your need. Now, along with your already extended left hand, you hold out your right hand palm upward and say, "What's it gonna take?"

You are offering a fair exchange, asking your loved one what a fair price would be. This is laying your goods down on the negotiation table and offering to trade.

This second step is a simple way to offer a fair exchange to your loved ones. Instead of begging, the second hand turns this into a transaction between two loving people as they exchange their needs.

The expectation in a marriage is that both partners want to meet their spouse's needs. No one wants their spouse to live an unfulfilled life. At the bare minimum, an unsatisfied spouse creates a miserable household and contributes to children at risk of detachment issues of their own.

If a person asks for sex or time together, it is highly unlikely their spouse will hold out their hand and say, "Okay, that will be five hundred dollars."

Rather, what is likely to happen is the spouse will do one of two things. They may say, "Yeah, I'd really like that too, but first _____." The other usual reaction is, "Okay, sure, I'd be happy to do that. Can you do _____ for me?"

Not only is this method a way to get your own needs met, but the explicit sharing of needs creates an opportunity to get to know your loved ones' needs. Someone who is shy about sharing their needs suddenly sees an open door as you invite them to share, while stating your own needs clearly as an example of how to communicate with trust.

Let's go back to the example used previously.

The vague communication of "Hey, how about we get some dinner and watch a movie tonight at seven o'clock?" turns into the following exchange:

Spouse 1: "Honey, I really feel disconnected from you lately because we haven't had much time together. I need to get some quality time with you. What's it gonna take to make that work?"

Spouse 2: "Oh, yeah, I've been feeling that way, too. Sorry, work's got me so stressed out. I already planned a night out tonight with coworkers to blow off some steam, but how about we spend all weekend together?"

Multiple things happened in this exchange:

- Spouse 1 clearly conveyed their unmet need and warned their partner the marriage is suffering for the lack of attention
- Spouse 1 did not apply blame or use guilt at all but simply stated the feeling they had and the circumstantial reasons
- Spouse 1 invited Spouse 2 to share their own needs and work together to solve the problem

- Spouse 1 conveyed trust that their partner will help them in good faith with this problem and not reject them
- Spouse 2 conveyed their hidden emotional state and environmental problems which contributed to the problem so Spouse 1 understood the distance was not personal
- Spouse 2 stated they felt the same need which unified the marriage as a team with similar goals
- Spouse 2 explained why existing plans take short-term priority over this request
- Spouse 2 assigned Spouse 1's needs as a high priority by dedicating an entire weekend to meeting their need

All of these benefits would have been missed without the explicit sharing of needs. Because the couple shared so openly, they now understand each other better, feel confident in their quality as partners, feel secure in the marriage, and both of their needs can be fulfilled.

And the entire conversation took them about ten seconds in total.

HOW DOES A HEALTHY RELATIONSHIP LOOK LONG-TERM?

This explicit sharing of needs creates a healthy flow between friends and partners. When just starting out, the two people may need to overcome resentment which has built up under the surface and festered under their wounds. Detached individuals will likely feel a surge of anxiety the first several times they contemplate opening up.

In time, if both parties follow this communication style and use it consistently, both issues should diminish. Resentment is released as needs are met and the detached individual realizes the other person truly wants to help them be fulfilled. Anxiety spikes decrease in severity and the length of procrastination between realizing the need and sharing it shortens as the detached person learns to trust their friends and family.

Perceived acceptance also begins to heal the detached individual. For the first time in their life, someone sees who they truly are on the inside. Instead of rejecting them, the trusted friend has embraced them more fully and continues to delight in their relationship. Confidence grows, and other mental health symptoms may diminish as the continuous stress on their mind diminishes or disappears entirely.

Both people will be able to comfortably share their needs the moment they feel them. Disappointments can be discussed not in terms of personal guilt but as opportunities to meet new needs and prove good intentions. Praise will feel genuine and come naturally as both parties are satisfied and content in their relationship.

In couples, they will cease to be two individuals living together and will instead become a unified partnership. Goals will be shared openly and the two can work together on solving shared problems. And all problems become shared, because the mutual fulfillment of needs becomes the highest priority.

As stated before, this form of explicit communication is not limited to just marriage. As the spouses learn this openness with each other, most seek this same level of emotional intimacy with their family and friends. Strong bonds are forged, misunderstandings are cleared away, and drama ceases to exist as explicit sharing of needs and clarity of intention creates immense trust and warmth.

CLARITY IS NECESSARY FOR INTIMACY

One additional issue can sometimes pop up which threatens this newfound intimacy. One tendency of detached individuals is to assume they know another person's thoughts, feelings, or intentions without asking. The worst is assumed and then reacted upon as if already confirmed.

When this issue arises, I advise detached individuals to learn the following skill:

When you find yourself becoming angry, upset, scared, or worried, stop and ask your friend, "Before I react, here is what I just heard. [Paraphrase how you interpreted what was just said]. Is that what you meant to say?"

Likely, your friend will react with horror and quickly say, "No! That's not what I meant!" Invite them to explain what was said, if they aren't already sputtering out what they really meant in a desperate frenzy to avoid your anger.

After they explain, take a deep breath and then react to the second statement. Trust your friend that the first statement was a complete misunderstanding and move on. Don't dwell on what was said or the troublesome phrasing.

Trust your friend. Don't pretend you can read their mind. And give them a chance to clarify before you attack.

PEOPLE WILL ABANDON YOU

The worst fears of the detached person are true: People will abandon you for this openness.

Yes, it's true.

People who've grown used to you never laying down boundaries will be angry when you suddenly tell them "No."

Detached people will see your openness and may run screaming from the anxiety your honesty provokes. They may call you all kinds of names as they flee from your vulnerability.

The truth is that vulnerability is not a weakness. Vulnerability takes control of a conversation and forces the other person to react to the openness. Either the person can choose to embrace the vulnerability and become vulnerable themselves, thus building an intimacy between the two parties, or they can reject the vulnerability and run in fear.

People with healthy skills and healthy attachment styles will see this level of explicit communication and openness and will surge forward into your life. An authentic and open person is a valuable asset to have in one's life because they can be trusted completely. No deception need be feared in relationships with them, and an honest person can expect their needs to be met through reciprocation and trade.

Explicit sharing of expectations and needs can weed out harmful people and act as a beacon to healthy people.

Your life will likely become filled and overflowing with loving relationships, true friends who know you and love you for who you are.

Loss of a few manipulative detached acquaintances becomes a small price to pay for genuine love.

WHAT IF I DON'T KNOW WHAT MY NEEDS ARE?

I get this question frequently in session. When a person has stuffed down their needs and desires for years on end they may forget how to even identify what it is they need.

The need for security often becomes fear which becomes anger, but all the person experiences consciously is the anger. The need for belonging twists into a form of fearful pre-rejection with the person experiencing an anxious aversion to the presence of others.

Because they only feel the surface emotions, the underlying needs are lost to their conscious mind.

There are many ways to get in touch with inner needs and discover what they are. One of the simplest ways is to identify negative emotions. These include anger, fear, sadness, and loneliness. A neutral state does not include these feelings, so it's a safe bet that an alteration has occurred wherein something has either been added or removed to create these negative feelings. Anger can be especially tricky because it prompts a person into action in order to feel powerful and may leave little time to pause and reflect.

How do we identify our negative feelings at the earliest stage and catch them in time to reflect and choose a new reaction? Physical warning signs are usually the easiest method. Anger is often accompanied by clenched fists, quick breathing, a rapid heartbeat, rising voice pitch and increasing volume, rigid muscles, and a defensive mindset of "me versus them." The goal of anger is usually to overpower feelings of being exposed and help the person feel more in control. Fear may have many of the same features, coupled with a desire for immediate removal from the situation. Sadness and loneliness, on the other hand, may become obvious through many symptoms including repeated sighing, a drooping physical posture, depressed mood, fatigue, loss of interest, or loss of the ability to feel pleasure. All of these may be accompanied by a strong desire to spend time with another person, though none of the people in your life may feel suitable.

If all else fails, ask your loved ones how you seem most often. Do you seem constantly angry but don't realize it?

A person experiencing anger, fear, sadness, or loneliness should ask themselves the following questions:

- If I'm angry, what other feelings might this anger be covering up?
- If I'm angry, what situations are frustrating me and why are they such a big deal to me? What am I afraid might happen?
- If I'm angry and the feeling stems from a perceived betrayal, what would it take for me to forgive that person and disperse the anger?
- If I'm lonely in my relationships, what sorts of connecting activities are missing?
- If I'm fearful, what would calm my concerns and help me feel more secure?
- If I'm sad, what would make me feel hopeful about the future?

Needs don't have to be purely reactive to negative moods, though. Needs can also be proactive. A person working to discover their hidden needs should ask themselves the following questions:

- What behavioral changes on both sides would it take for me to feel satisfied in my relationships?

- How often do I want physical intimacy, and what forms do I crave besides sex?
- When I come home from being out, what do I want most?
- When I feel stressed, what calms me down?
- When I think of having a perfect day, what activities do I see myself doing?
- How much quality time in a week do I require with my loved ones to feel close and connected?
- How much alone time in a week do I require by myself to feel calm and centered?
- What activities such as crafts, art, sports, or other forms of mental engagement give me pleasure? How often do I need to engage in these activities to feel that life has genuinely positive aspects?

CHAPTER 8
Pursuing Perfection

Living with insecurity has a tendency to smother you with an absolute demand to be perfect.

Insecure people worry that by being imperfect they risk losing the love of everyone around them. Any perceived imperfection, no matter how small, becomes their worst enemy. The goal then is to be perfect at all times

Just to put in perspective how impossible this is, the insecure person believes that they have to be born absolutely perfect and flawless in every skill, craft, profession, and field of knowledge. There can be no practice time where they slowly develop a skill and get better or learning period where they study and gain knowledge. They must know and be able to perform every act imaginable with flawless precision.

This is what I called expecting perfection. They expect themselves to be perfect right now.

Right. Now.

There is no time allowed for learning or practicing or getting better. Immediate perfection. Anything less risks everything they love and care about.

The healthy person does not expect perfection. Instead, they pursue perfection. When they make a mistake, they figure out what it would take to be perfect at that task. This might mean looking to mentors for solutions, or reading a book. They give themselves a chance to learn and practice. They do not expect themselves to have everything mastered the moment they hear about it.

One of the best ways to make this shift is simply by acknowledging that it is impossible to be born absolutely perfect in every capacity. Recognizing the ridiculous standard to which you are holding yourself is often the most effective means of breaking this pattern. Give yourself at least a little bit of time to learn.

Tell yourself the following affirmations out loud:

"It is okay that I'm not perfect right now."

"Every time I practice, I get better."

"Someday I will be great, but to become great, I have to practice first."

"It is okay to not be perfect as long as I am learning and getting better."

Write these down on sticky notes or on your bathroom mirror and read them out loud to yourself every day when you're getting ready. Stick them to your computer monitor to glance at while editing your creative works. Write them on the back of your hand so they're with you all day.

If you are not learning successfully, do not assume you're a complete idiot but rather assume that you are not learning in the right way. Seek out a teacher who can help you learn.

Pursuing perfection looks like this: you find a deficiency in some skill or area of knowledge. So you set out to fix that. You practice the skill until you are good at it, or you search out sources of knowledge to learn about that gap in your education. The goal is to perfect yourself down the line, in the distant future, because you will never really be perfect at everything. Instead, you are seeking mastery in the various pursuits in your life. You will leapfrog forward throughout your life until others believe you to be the pinnacle of achievement in your field. Even so, you will still find flaws and seek to sharpen a skill so fine that only you can see the distinction.

By expecting perfection now, an insecure individual will run screaming from every task, craft, or activity which requires any level of practice. They will never develop real skills in which they can have pride. This is part of staying insecure, because they will never really achieve anything.

By allowing yourself to be imperfect now for the sake of becoming a master later, you can actually build real achievements.

Do not expect perfection, but pursue it relentlessly.

CHAPTER 9
Help, something went wrong!

Invariably, individuals recovering from lifelong insecurity will hit speed bumps in their journey toward health.

The speed bumps can sometimes derail the entire effort for days on end as the insecure individual grapples with their own brain. "I told you this was a bad idea!" their brain shouts at them as they swirl into a vortex of despair and anxiety.

This usually happens when the insecure person encounters an unhealthy person, or a new situation with which they are not yet familiar. Something throws them off their usual pace and they struggle with the new environment or scenario. The issue is that their brain has not generalized the new skills into these unusual environments yet.

There's a process called **systematic desensitization**, which is just a fancy way of saying that if you do something over and over it eventually becomes mundane and boring. Even the most anxiety-provoking situation, if done frequently enough with the right set of skills, can become a boring activity which evokes no emotional response whatsoever.

Now, this does not mean that new situations will not evoke emotional responses, only situations exactly like the one encountered. Each new variable which changes that setting becomes a new object for your brain to learn to handle.

Imagine your brain is a very skittish dog on a leash. Everywhere you take your dog he barks and barks and gets nervous at everything that's new. You have to acclimate him to the grocery store, and you do this by going step-by-step through each department. First the deli, with all the meat grinders and people standing at the counter. Next is the bakery with all the smells and trays of rolls. Next is the freezer section which is very cold and confuses him. Then the pharmacy where people are talking loudly about medications. Last is the checkout line, perhaps the most stressful of all where he must stand in close proximity to other people as machines beep and objects are thrown in rattling bags.

You can tell your dog that this is all the same grocery store, but to him each department is a new experience and is newly frightening. And this is just one store! After he's acclimated to the grocery store, that doesn't mean he'll be just fine at the shopping mall. You need to get him used to each store in the mall.

Now apply this to your brain. You may get very used to sharing new skills with your close friends but then try to share them with your family and freak out. This doesn't mean the skills were garbage. It just means you're not used to the new situation yet. However, as you share this open communication with your family and receive the same acceptance as with your friends, your brain may begin to do something called **generalizing**. This means that other situations which are similar may evoke the same expectation in your brain, rather than freaking out about it being slightly different.

You will also make mistakes. Many times over the course of your life you will make mistakes that will cause you to cringe and send you running back into the cycle of worry.

If you thought you were going to escape insecurity forever, then here, have some despair.

Remember that the goal is not to expect perfection, but to pursue it. As you make mistakes, learn from them! Your mistakes will be valuable lessons to help you sharpen yourself in the direction you want to go. When you're worried or nervous, acknowledge it. Seek out a friend you can share it with. Confront the person you made the mistake with and apologize. Own the mistake and ask for a way to make it right. Make amends, and move on with your life.

Your returns to anxiety are actually opportunities for you to spread those new skills across your brain. When you feel yourself growing anxious, stop. Ask yourself what it is that's making you feel that way. Congratulations, you found a new area to improve yourself! You are not back at square one, but entering new territory that needs to be reclaimed.

Feeling anxiety is actually an opportunity for you to grow in confidence and refine the person that you are into the person you want to be.

Learn to embrace the speed bumps as opportunities to grow. Then you don't need to dread temporary relapses into insecure behaviors.

FINAL THOUGHTS

Once a person has begun slaying their fear and creating greater intimacy in their relationships, they often experience a desperate fear that they're going to somehow ruin everything. "Intimacy is great," they think, "but now that I know what I've been missing, I'm afraid I'm going to screw it all up with one really horrible mistake!"

The bad news is that, yes, you will make a mistake. You will make many mistakes. And the people with whom you've created the reciprocal sharing should point out your mistakes and give you a chance to make things right. That's precisely the point of this entire exercise and the reason for developing intimacy.

Do not live in fear that your honest mistakes will destroy every scrap of intimacy. So long as your mistakes are not malicious or born of distrust, other people are generally quick to forgive. That's why your past mistakes have been so costly: they revealed a lack of desire to stay connected to others or came from outright malice as you attacked in petty anger. The purpose in building a new life full of intimacy is that both sides in your relationships now agree to put the wellbeing of the relationship above pride or emotion and to work together in navigating mistakes and misunderstandings with the explicit goal of keeping the relationship intact. The goal is to keep the relationship alive forever, indefinitely, until the end of your lives. From such a starting place, any honest mistake is just a speed bump on a road expected to run on without end.

Detached individuals who are married usually begin by opening up to their spouse. As the detached person becomes attached to their spouse, I encourage them to spread out to other relationships and develop intimacy with friends and family. The average person only needs a few intimate relationships to begin feeling safe and secure in the world. Confidence often begins to grow rapidly after a person has been accepted by just two or three others. You should no longer crave validation from everyone you meet because you will have the total acceptance and lasting love of your closest companions. No matter what happens, you can believe you are loved and have a place to go where you are accepted and wanted.

Slaying Your Fear is by no means an exhaustive guide to every situation a person with attachment issues may face. Instead, I hope this book helps each reader find the courage to begin traveling a lifelong road toward fulfillment and peace in their life. To those eager for more reading material on the subject of attachments and healing I enthusiastically recommend *No More Mr. Nice Guy: A Proven Plan for Getting What You Want in Love, Sex, and Life* by Dr. Robert A. Glover. The book is available on Amazon and several resources are available on his website at DrGlover.com. For detached individuals seeking guidance specifically in their marriage, my book *Exhausted Wives, Bewildered Husbands* is available on Amazon.

Any reader who feels they may suffer from diagnosable concerns or whose issues are impacting their daily living and leading to feelings of depression is enormously encouraged to find a qualified mental health professional such as a therapist to assess the concerns and help find specific solutions useful to the individual. An excellent resource for this is PsychologyToday.com where readers can find helpful search tools to locate mental health professionals by zip code.

The skills shared in this book may not be the direct solution to every problem an insecure person will face, but the mindset cultivated by practicing these skills can be used to navigate any situation and find the necessary solution. As people communicate more explicitly, intimacy grows. As intimacy develops in relationships, the individual can blossom into a fulfilled person and realize their own deepest potential.

Reader, you've learned the necessary skills to go forth and slay your fear. Get your own fears out of the way and open up to those around you. Build the life you've always longed for.

Emotional security is only a few practiced skills away.

ABOUT THE AUTHOR

Adam Lane Smith is a retired licensed psychotherapist specialized in trauma and attachment with experience in both clinical and correctional mental health settings. That includes his work in the California justice system where he treated inmates facing the death penalty and in a clinical setting treating couples, millionaire entrepreneurs, CEOs, investors, first responders, and military families. Adam terminated his therapist license to consult internationally and expand global awareness about attachment. He has appeared on numerous podcasts discussing generational attachment issues, recovering from trauma, and repairing attachment. For more information check out his website at AdamLaneSmith.com or email him at Info@AdamLaneSmith.com.

Made in the USA
Monee, IL
09 March 2023

Made in the USA
Monee, IL
09 March 2023